OPPORTUNITIES

in

10104

Photography
Careers

OPPORTUNITIES

in

Photography
Careers

REVISED EDITION

BERVIN JOHNSON, ROBERT E. MAYER, AND FRED SCHMIDT

VGM Career Books

New York   Chicago   San Francisco   Lisbon   London   Madrid   Mexico City
Milan   New Delhi   San Juan   Seoul   Singapore   Sydney   Toronto

The *McGraw·Hill* Companies

Library of Congress Cataloging-in-Publication Data

Johnson, Bervin M.
    Opportunities in photography careers / Bervin Johnson, Robert E. Mayer, and Fred
Schmidt.— Rev. ed.
        p.   cm. — (VGM opportunities series)
    ISBN 0-07-143723-1
    1. Photography—Vocational guidance.   I. Mayer, Robert E.   II. Schmidt,
Fred.   III. Title.   IV. Series.

TR154.J64   2004
770'.023—dc22   2004006226

1 2 3 4 5 6 7 8 9 0   DOC/DOC   3 2 1 0 9 8 7 6 5 4

ISBN 0-07-143723-1

Interior design by Rattray Design

McGraw-Hill books are available at special quantity discounts to use as premiums and
sales promotions, or for use in corporate training programs. For more information, please
write to the Director of Special Sales, Professional Publishing, McGraw-Hill, Two Penn
Plaza, New York, NY 10121-2298. Or contact your local bookstore.

This book is printed on acid-free paper.

To our photographic mentors—the sharing, caring, knowledgeable individuals who help novice photographers become more proficient in the profession.

This book is dedicated to the late Clarence H. White Jr., instructor, friend, and mentor. As an instructor at Ohio University in the 1950s, Clarence was an inspiration to all of his many photography students. He taught us to use photography creatively as a means of communication in a visually oriented world. His sage advice and guidance shaped students into true professionals, ready for any facet of photography they would pursue in later years.

CONTENTS

Knocking on doors. Writing application letters. Using advertising to get employment. Advantages of a career in photography. Earning potential.

technology. Photography as art. Federal government.
Film and television. Opportunities in teaching.

Foreword

Is it true that a picture is worth a thousand words? Millions of people must think so, because photography plays a tremendously important part in our everyday lives.

Anyone can use a simple camera, and most people do. This means that amateur photography is big business, creating jobs for thousands of photographic technicians and others who work in manufacturing, sales, and processing industries.

At the other end of the spectrum from hobbyists and proud parents taking snapshots are professional photographers who pursue a variety of creative and challenging careers. Pick up a newspaper or magazine and you will see photos. Read a book, look at a CD cover, open a school yearbook, drive by a billboard advertisement . . . photographs are used everywhere. These professional photographers, using more complex equipment and taking advantage of greater knowledge than amateurs, fulfill a wide range of jobs that are often hidden from the general public. Most people are aware of the portrait photographers who make images of us at various times in our lives; but many people don't think of the photojournalists and the biomedical, industrial, scientific, and commercial photographers who advertise or illustrate what goes on in our society.

Almost no one thinks about the individuals who designed or manufactured the films we use or who are responsible for the processing and printing when the film has been shot. These photofinishing careers demand individuals with highly specialized skills and the creativity necessary to solve complex problems that face the photographic industry. In the past few years, there has been a major shift toward computer imaging, which places new demands upon those involved with this side of the business.

Working as a photographer or as a photofinisher requires special training and abilities. If you are interested in the possibility of following a career related to these exciting professions, this book should prove quite helpful. It provides key information you will need to pursue such a career. The authors have outlined details you will need about the types of jobs available, job expectations, background and education needed, and other factors involved in a career. You're encouraged to use this book as an introduction to the job possibilities in this creative and challenging area. Perhaps your future holds a career behind the camera or in an equally important support role.

Robert Heist Jr., Chairman
Department of Photographic Technology
Randolph Community College
Asheboro, North Carolina

Acknowledgments

No book covering as wide a range of material as this one could have been completed without the help of friends, colleagues, and experts in every area imaginable. To all of them, our gratitude is deep and warm. This career volume is truly a cooperative effort.

Special thanks to Douglas Stewart for the section on teaching. Thanks also to the following for reviewing and suggesting updates: Les Stroebel for sections on scientific and technical photography, Nile Root for biomedical photography, Will Counts for photojournalism, Don Beyer for industrial photography, Jerry Cornelius for commercial photography, and Terry Klondaris for portrait photography.

Thanks also to the following: American Society of Media Photographers; Brooks Institute of Photography; Cathy Hefferin, Dakota County Technical College; Evidence Photographers International Council; Ithaca College; National Press Photographers Association; Photomarketing Association International; Randolph Community College; Rocky Mountain School of Photography; U.S. Department of Labor.

1

Importance of Photography

In the modern world, probably no other medium has more impact on everyday life than photography. We are influenced by visuals of all types, everywhere. Television, newspapers, magazines, the Internet, and books all use photography extensively to tell a story or capture our attention. Even the images in advertisements help convince us we need a product or service.

No subject is too distant or too minute to photograph. Faraway stars and planets, as well as the ocean floor and the world of microbes, are all explored and recorded with cameras of various types. Digital photography is revolutionizing the industry at this very moment and will continue to do so. Images invisible to the eye are recorded clearly with the aid of infrared and ultraviolet films. Metals of all types are x-rayed in detail for observation and future use. The insides of human bodies have been x-rayed for many years; CAT scans and MRIs produce color x-rays and cross-section profiles of the human body.

Millions of people throughout the world cannot read, and few people can read and comprehend more than 250 words per minute. As a result, photography has taken a leading role in communications. Regardless of the source of the original image (real life, art, dramatic staging), it is almost inevitable that eventually it passes through some means of photographic process. With the aid of machinery and electronics, the visual image has a decided edge over the written word. Furthermore, the mind is capable of assimilating visual input faster than it can assimilate the spoken or written word.

America's space program has been using photography from its beginning to record events and fascinate the world's population with images of outer space. The quality of detail and speed of electronic transmission back to earth are indications that the future of photography is virtually limitless. In recent years, we have all been captivated by the images of the rocky, red surface of Mars taken by cameras mounted on roving vehicles as well as stunning images sent back from unmanned space probes on their journeys through the solar system. The resulting pictures have expanded our knowledge of the universe.

The public is visually motivated in everything it does and sees. Television, music videos, movies, streaming video on the Internet, and printed photographs in our magazines and textbooks leave a lasting visual impression on everyone. Today people grow up with and are being educated with visual images.

The United States leads the world in picture taking, with about three-fourths of the nation's families owning at least one camera. Packing a camera (whether a film camera or digital) is almost the first step in preparing for a vacation trip. Americans are such avid picture makers that more than two million rolls of film are exposed each day (97 percent of which are color), and approximately 180,000 pictures are taken every hour.

Our high standard of living reflects the effectiveness of photography as it is used to appeal to our desires. Unconsciously we are sold cars, homes, food, fashions, and vacation trips to beautiful lands through photographic illustrations used in magazines, newspapers, television, the Internet, billboards, and movies.

Not only is photography a hobby for countless people, but it is also a major source of entertainment. Millions of people spend hours upon hours enjoying films and videos in their homes and in theaters. Pictures are used to teach people how to do things and to convey information and ideas. Schools and colleges, business and industry are using more and more images to advertise and to convey their messages.

The part photography plays in mass communication has increased so much in our lifetimes because of the efficiency of transmission and duplication. Whether one or ten million copies of any given photograph are needed, mass distribution is easy. The technologies of photography have been so simplified that if you walk into any toy store, you will see cameras that take photos of surprising quality that have been manufactured and marketed specifically for very young children.

With remote camera–satellites whirling millions of miles out in space and with the sales and use of digital cameras exploding in the marketplace, who knows what the future will bring in such a popular and diversified field as photography?

History of Photography

The word *photography* derives from Greek words meaning "light" and "writing." The first experimental attempts at real photography were not undertaken until 1802, at which time Thomas Wedgwood, an English scientist, made photographic copies of paintings and worked with Sir Humphrey Davy in the production of silhouettes. Both Wedgwood and Davy made unsuccessful attempts to produce photographs of objects by means of a simple camera. Their early experiments were hampered by not knowing how to make pictures permanent.

In 1827 the French inventor Joseph Nicéphore Niépce made the first photograph, or *heliograph* ("sun writing"). He left his camera obscura—a large box with a tiny opening in one side that admitted light—sitting for eight hours collecting rays of light; he then projected them onto a pewter plate coated with bitumen of Judea, a light-sensitive chemical. He washed the plate in lavender oil and petroleum. On the plate remained an image of the roof and walls of his barn in the village of Saint-Loup-de-Varennes.

Daguerreotypes and Glass Plates

Daguerreotypes were developed in 1829 when Niépce joined with fellow French inventor Louis Daguerre to develop this remarkable achievement in photography. The big drawback to this new process was that no copies could be made from the plates. The first multiple printing came about in 1840, when the British inventor William Henry Fox Talbot introduced the calotype process, which produced a negative from light-sensitive paper.

The concern of improving negative quality led to the discovery of photographic glass plates in 1847 by Claude Felix Niépce de Saint Victor. To make a photograph, the glass plate was coated with a mixture of silver salts and wet emulsion. The plate had to remain moist during exposure and developing, requiring that photographs be processed immediately after being taken.

Samuel F. B. Morse, inventor of the telegraph, contributed much to the progress of photography through his experimentations with daguerreotypes after the details of the process arrived in America in 1839. In fact, many gave him credit as being the father of American photography. He became one of the first instructors of photography, and among his many students was Matthew B. Brady, without a doubt the most famous American photographer of the nineteenth century. Brady developed a lucrative photography business with studios in New York and Philadelphia, which he later abandoned to photograph the Civil War. At the end of the war, Brady had a collection of 7,000 glass plates, including 30 he had made of Abraham Lincoln. He and his crew made these between the years 1860 and 1864. At that time, there were no extensive markets for his war pictures because newspapers and magazines had no way of reproducing them except by expensive engravings made by artists copying his photographs.

After the American Civil War, camera reporters began to show an interest in covering the growth of the frontier from the Mississippi River to the Rocky Mountains. Probably the most famous photographer of this movement was William Henry Jackson, who loaded a camera big enough to use 20″ × 24″ glass plates on a mule's back and joined the Hayden survey in 1875. Other mules were loaded with more cameras, lenses, glass plates, chemicals, trays, dark tents, and water for exploring the region now known as Yellowstone National Park. Jackson's scenic photographs of this area were used as the principal evidence in persuading Congress to establish the nation's first national park. During the time that Jackson was photographing the wonders of Yellowstone, the British physician R. L. Maddox developed a light-sensitive gelatin emulsion that could dry on a plate without damaging the silver salts. Dry plates did not require immediate processing and thus offered freedom from the burden of the traveling darkroom.

Newspaper Photographs

The first newspaper halftone appeared in 1880 in the *New York Daily Graphic*. Along with the improvement of printing processes, the stature of the photographer also improved because of the distribution of photographs to thousands of viewers. With this sudden public exposure came a greater demand for photographs of all types. Studios became more numerous, and tremendous technical developments were made in all fields of photography. Because of the increasing demand for this new form of communication in a society of increasing complexity, the photographic industry emerged and blossomed, branching into specialized fields like portraiture, commercial photography, publication photography, photofinishing, and the manufacturing and sales of photographic supplies.

Photography for the Public

Any discussion of photography should include mention of George Eastman, the first manufacturer in the United States to formulate and put into practice large-scale camera production at low costs for the world market. It can truthfully be said that for more than 100 years progress in photography went hand in hand with the history and growth of the Eastman Kodak Company.

George Eastman, an American dry-plate manufacturer, advertised in 1884 that "shortly will be introduced a new sensitive film which is believed will prove an economical and convenient substitute for glass dry plates both for outdoor and studio work." This flexible, transparent film, plus an apparatus built simultaneously by American inventor Thomas Edison, made motion pictures successful.

In 1888 Eastman introduced the first Kodak camera. It was a box-type camera, lightweight and small, loaded with a stripping paper long enough for 100 exposures. The price of the camera loaded with film was $25. The camera and exposed film had to be shipped to Rochester, New York, to have the film removed and processed into prints and another strip of film loaded into the camera. The cost for this service was $10. The Kodak camera created an entirely new market and brought forth the phrase, "You press the button and we do the rest." Thus photography was simplified to the point where anyone could take pictures with a handheld camera simply by pressing a button.

The Kodak Company also made notable contributions to photography in the medical, scientific, educational, and entertainment fields. The introduction of Kodachrome color transparency film in 1935 revitalized the world of photography. Further improvements in films contributed much to the progress of the television industry, the data processing field, and space projects. Since 1935, improved products have continued to evolve in the United States, Europe, and Japan. Users of both still and motion picture film and equipment continue to benefit from these product improvements.

Photography Today

Rapid developments in lighting, lenses, films, cameras, developers, and selling techniques advanced the photographer and the photographic profession significantly over the past several decades. Direct color photography is now used in all media and is in constant demand by the buying public. (Other chapters of this book will go into more detail concerning the many types of photography and classifications of photographers.)

Advances in color emulsion technology have produced many brands of color slide and color negative films with normal ISO speeds of 1,600 ASA or more. A mere 30 years ago, even the fastest black-and-white films were only 400 ASA. These new films have broadened the appeal of amateur cameras that can produce an acceptable picture anywhere under any type of lighting.

During the 1980s, 35mm lens/shutter compact cameras, which accounted for about half of all cameras sold in the United States, and the growth of one-hour minilabs were the big trends. The marketplace was still enjoying the relatively recent innovation of autofocus cameras—which relieved the user of the need both to focus and to choose a shutter speed—when digital cameras came on the scene. The recent leap to digital technology, which came in so short a time, has had a tremendous impact on the world of film. Film is replaced with a chip, on which hundreds of images can be stored, for later transfer to a computer or CD. From there, images can be manipulated and printed—if they are printed at all—either at home on photo-quality paper or at a store where that printing service is provided.

Electronics are an increasingly integral part of photography as we know it today: in cameras, accessories, and processing laboratories. New developments in the technology of cameras, scanners, computers, and other types of equipment continue to change the ways photographs and other types of information are produced, distributed, and used. New job opportunities and job descriptions are being developed. Anyone entering the field of photography today will find it ever-changing and improving. One only needs to think of the high-speed motion picture cameras and the increasing number of photos appearing on the Internet, or the high-quality, close-up photographs made of Mars and Saturn and other planets, to get an idea of the impact photography is making on mass communications and the growing visual consciousness among people.

Employment of Photographers

According to the U.S. Department of Labor, about 139,000 people are employed as photographers in the United States. Some of the areas in which they hold jobs include the following:

Commercial photography	Photojournalism
Media photography	Television production
Portrait photography	Movie production
Scientific photography	Artistic photography

About four out of ten photographers are self-employed, which is a higher proportion than the average for all occupational areas. Many of those who are self-employed operate their own portrait studios or other small businesses specializing in photography. Some work on a freelance or contract basis for advertising agencies, magazines, website development specialists, portrait studios, police departments, or stock photo agencies. (See Appendix A for organizations that deal with these specialties.)

Salaried photographers work in a variety of areas. Employers include the following:

Photography studios	Advertising agencies
Newspapers	Public relations firms
Magazines	Government agencies

Many jobs are salaried, and qualified individuals work a normal 35- to 40-hour week. The demand for commercial and portrait photographers remains relatively constant today. While some learn their skills by on-the-job training, more and more still photographers, especially those working for major firms as industrial photographers, must have advanced academic degrees in photography, or at least have graduated from one- or two-year practical-training courses.

Salaries

Salaries earned by photographers vary widely. Earnings differ by field of specialty, geographical area, experience, and other factors.

According to the National Press Photographers Association (NPPA), beginning salaries in the newspaper field range from $250 to $300 per week or $13,000 to $15,600 annually. Experienced newspaper photographers may earn more than twice that amount.

According to the NPPA, pay in the television field averages about $500 per week after five years of experience, or $26,000 yearly. Photographers at larger newspapers and television stations tend to earn higher salaries than those serving smaller markets.

The U.S. Department of Labor reports that the average yearly salary for photographers and camera operators falls between $25,000 and $30,000. Some earn less than $15,000 a year, while others earn $50,000 or more.

Because circumstances vary so widely (one photographer might operate a lucrative studio in Beverly Hills, while another works for a small-town newspaper in rural Montana), "average" salaries have limited meaning when it comes to working in this field. Probably the best advice is to check with employers of photographers (or with practicing photographers) in your area and ask what income ranges are common. That way you'll get a feel for salaries that might be expected. Scanning the want ads can sometimes provide similar information.

Canadian Outlook

We spoke with several professional photographers in Canada who commented that there are lots of opportunities for photographers there, especially around major population centers. They said there is always a demand for qualified photo lab technicians.

One Canadian photo writer said there are always opportunities for skilled and experienced photographers who know what they are doing. Since the population is smaller than that of the United States, and there are fewer firms using photography, competition is tougher. Canadian photographers have to generalize more to serve a broader client base and not try to be specialists in just one type of photography.

The Professional Photographers of Canada is an active group of professionals that was formed in 1946 by a group of commercial and press photographers. They share their photographic expertise through a bilingual publication called *enVISION*, published six times a year, and an annual convention. They also have an excellent website at ppoc.ca. There are six provincial chapters throughout Canada, and they, too, host events and conventions. You should be able to obtain current and pertinent advice from local members of this group to assist you in finding schooling or employment in the field of photography in Canada.

2

LEARNING THE CRAFT

LIKE ANY OTHER craft that includes creative skill as well as knowledge, photography has no hard-and-fast rules for success. However, some clues can be obtained from observing the traits of contemporary photographers in the way they work and live.

Patience, persistence, an inquisitive mind, enthusiasm, a desire to learn, creativity, and a genuine interest in nearly everything are the major personal qualifications for getting started in photography. Good people skills are also important. Seriousness of purpose and a willingness to assume greater responsibilities are attributes that do not go unnoticed when advancement opportunities arise.

If you are interested in a basic 40-hour workweek, doing some detailed operation for an established photographic business or industrial photography department, you do not need to have a great amount of ambition. But you should have a goal or dream to be the best photographer in your school, in your community, in your state, or in your professional associations to get to the top in your field.

When you feel this way about your work, you will find it fun and enjoyable and your livelihood then ceases to feel like work.

Dependability is another key to success. In the photographic profession, many appointments and deadlines must be met and completed on time. Willingness to give service is most important in choosing photography as a profession. Working long hours, late at night, weekends, and some Sundays and holidays is often necessary to become successful in many fields of photography. Attendance at conventions and seminars, as well as taking advantage of refresher courses, is important to keep up with trends, new products, and technical developments in the photographic world.

You will progress faster in most areas of photography by being artistically inclined or having some art background. To go to the top, a photographer needs to know the basics of photography, as well as something about computers and the Internet, bookkeeping, purchasing, electronics, optics, graphic reproduction, color, architecture, anatomy, lighting, advertising, public relations, and psychology. In addition, a person should have a well-rounded knowledge of what is going on in the community, the nation, and the world.

In no other profession or trade could you find such a diversified and interesting challenge. If you want to know about all these things and are enthusiastic about doing them, you should go far. Your chances of finding success and enjoyment in photography are greater if you possess these attributes.

Professional organizations are placing increased emphasis upon educational programs. Manufacturers and distributors are making contributions and working with educational institutions in developing new courses in photography. Upgrading curricula, textbooks, equipment, and faculties is recognized as a top priority project by all.

Approaches to Training

Any student contemplating enrolling in any advanced course in photography should be aware that there are two general approaches. Professionally oriented programs are structured to prepare the students to produce still or motion pictures according to the requirements specified by their clients or employers. Other courses have a fine arts basis of instruction. The latter help the individuals sharpen their artistic and creative visions rather than teach them how to produce images to meet commercial needs.

Both types of courses tend to provide students with an academic background in the fundamentals of photography, its history, and current processes and various methods necessary to produce photographic images. The obvious differences arc in the final use of the photographs produced, or who pays for the prints.

In general, community colleges and trade schools tend to offer more technical courses where most of the work is related to the major subject area of photography. Conversely, students who attend four-year colleges or universities only have one-fourth to one-third of their courses in their major (photography) area. The bulk of the additional credit courses are in other subjects, such as the humanities, sciences, mathematics, communications, and various electives. A graduate from a four-year program generally has a broader, more diversified background, but it takes two additional years and more tuition to achieve this diversification, and the individual will enter the job market later to begin earning a living.

There are many specializations within the separate fields of motion pictures and video, still photography, and graphic arts. Most students entering a vocational field seldom are aware of the variety of jobs and specializations available to graduates. A list of the various positions filled by recent graduates of photographic programs may be helpful. Since any one of these areas of specialization may not be in great demand several years in the future, it would be wise to take courses that overlap whenever possible.

More than a thousand schools offer courses in photography. A small sample of them is given in Appendix B. Whether you are in high school or are established in a different career and contemplating a change to the photography profession, you have an important decision to make: can you afford the time and cost of getting as much academic education as possible before pursuing a lifetime career? If you decide you can afford it, this list of schools for photographic training will be worth your writing to get additional information concerning their courses and costs.

Due to the rapid pace at which photography is moving today as a communications medium, combined with the spiraling cost of everything in general, it is difficult to offer an accurate idea of the costs for courses offered by various schools. In general, a wide selection of education offerings are available to those interested in learning various aspects of the craft. For example, a one-day "Flying Short Course" is given each year in selected localities by the National Press Photographers Association (nppa.org); refresher courses of various lengths are offered through the year at the Winona International School of Professional Photography in Atlanta, Georgia (ohwy.com); evening courses are offered by adult education programs in or near most communities; and curricula leading to the highest academic degrees are available at many colleges and universities.

Some high schools offer courses in photography and some have full-fledged programs. For example, Abraham Lincoln High School in San Jose (lincolnhighsanjose.org) offers an advanced multimedia program that includes an emphasis on digital photography. But in most cases, you will need to study at a trade or technical school, community college, or university to earn a degree or diploma in photography.

Because many photographic curricula are adapted to accept whatever the particular department has in the way of related subjects and instructors, there is no model or standard curriculum for photography education. To help prospective students of photography and counselors in advising them on curricula being offered, we will use the following institutions as examples: Dakota County Technical College, Milwaukee Area Technical College, Hallmark Institute of Photography, Rochester Institute of Technology's School of Photographic Arts and Sciences, and Brooks Institute of Photography.

Community and Technical Colleges

Directories, available in some school and public libraries, contain the names and addresses of many community and junior colleges with requirements for admission to each college, enrollment, descriptions of the campus facilities, curricula offered, costs, and financial aid available. One example is *Peterson's Two-Year Colleges*.

There is a wide variety of courses in photography offered at community and technical colleges. Typically, these programs offer basic courses that are less expensive to take than those at four-year colleges and universities.

Dakota County Technical College

A good example of a comprehensive photography program at the community college level is the program offered by Dakota County Technical College (dctc.mnscu.edu) in Rosemount, Minnesota. This college offers five different programs related to photography.

The programs range in length from a two-year, associate-degree program requiring the completion of 64 credits to a short (16-credit) certificate program. Following is an overview of the requirements of each program and the courses offered.

Evening courses are offered in beginning though advanced photography, photo processing, and electronic imaging. Students can achieve certificates, a diploma, or a degree in photography by participating in an evening-track sequence.

A.A.S. Degree, Photographing Imaging Technology

Required credits: 64 (44 required technical credits and 20 general education credits)

Courses Include
Introduction to Visual Communications
Introduction to Photoshop
Introduction to Photography
Introduction to QuarkXPress
Introduction to Illustrator
Lighting Techniques
Basic Processing and Monitoring
Copy and Restoration
Introduction to Custom Printing
Machine Printing Systems
Custom Color Printing
Portrait Photography
Introduction to Digital Imaging
VisCom Career/Portfolio Development
Commercial Photography
Digital Photography
Digital Darkroom

Photography on the Internet
Business Presentations
Portfolio Development (Photo Careers)

Diploma, Photographic Imaging Technology

Required credits: 34 (31 required technical credits and 3 general education credits)

Courses Include
Introduction to Visual Communications
Introduction to Photoshop
Introduction to Photography
Lighting Techniques
Basic Processing and Monitoring
Copy and Restoration
Introduction to Custom Printing
Machine Printing Systems
Custom Color Printing
Portrait Photography
Introduction to Digital Imaging
VisCom Career/Portfolio Development
Portfolio Development (Photo Careers)

Certificate, Photojournalism

Total required credits: 26 (19 required technical credits, 1 technical elective credit, and 6 general education credits)

Courses Include
Introduction to Visual Communications
Introduction to Photoshop

Introduction to Photography
Introduction to QuarkXPress
Lighting Techniques
Reporting
Photojournalism
VisCom Career/Portfolio Development
Portfolio Development (Photo Careers)
VisCom Internship

Certificate, Digital Imaging Technician

Total required technical credits: 24 (21 required technical credits and 3 technical electives)

Courses Include
Introduction to Visual Communications
Introduction to Photoshop
Introduction to Photography
Printing Lab I
Introduction to QuarkXPress
Introduction to Illustrator
Introduction to Digital Imaging
Digital Darkroom
Business Presentations
Portfolio Development (Photo Careers)

Certificate, Photographer Assistant

Total required technical credits: 16

Courses Include
Introduction to Photoshop
Introduction to Photography

Printing Lab I
Photography for Profit
Photography Workshop
Lighting Techniques
Portrait Photography
Commercial Photography
Portfolio Development

Milwaukee Area Technical College

The Milwaukee Area Technical College (MATC) also has an impressive photography program. Recent program offerings at MATC (milwaukee.tec.wi.us) include the following:

Fundamental Photography
Survey of Digital Photography
Digital Photography
Digital Color Management for the Graphic Industry
View Camera Techniques
Photographic Trends
Photographic Lighting
Photographic Portfolio
Commercial Photography
Portraiture
Advanced Studio Lighting
Photographic Machine and Process Monitoring
Measurement Techniques
Color Photography I and II
Communicating with Color Photography
Digital Video and Still Photography
Candid and Formal Wedding Photography
Photo Journalism

Industrial Photography
Photographic Internship
Basic Photography
Darkroom Techniques
Moving Image Photography

Trade Schools

Technical and trade schools have more specialized curricula than community colleges. They are streamlined and free of the usual academic studies normally a part of photography courses in colleges and universities. In these schools, you learn by doing and working under the immediate supervision of an instructor.

Trade schools seem to be growing in popularity, since there are increasing numbers of them across the country. The mere fact that students receive more intensive training, and therefore complete their training in one or two years, is appealing to many individuals with a desire to learn photography but with a limited budget for schooling.

To obtain a better idea of the types of vocational training currently available, look online or ask a research librarian for help finding out what directories are available to you. Pertinent categories listed under photography schools and courses include:

Digital Photography
Photo Equipment Technician
Photographic Technician
Photography
Photography and Film Communications
Photography Commercial/Professional
Photo Lab Technician
Photojournalism

Hallmark Institute of Photography

The Hallmark Institute of Photography (http://hallmark.edu) in Turner Falls, Massachusetts, is one school that provides specialized photographic training in only 10 months. Hallmark takes pride in its atmosphere of real-world experience in photography, which is structured more as a photographer/client relationship rather than as student/teacher.

Hallmark offers an intensive schedule requiring student attendance and involvement on a Monday-through-Friday, full-day basis, with occasional evening and weekend assignments. To complete this accelerated program, a cumulative total of approximately 1,400 class hours in 40 weeks is required, which is said to be the equivalent of nearly two years of traditional academic schedules. Although about 65 percent of this class time is related to the art and techniques of photography (both traditional and digital), the remainder is devoted to the business of photography, with courses in areas such as business management, marketing, finance, and personnel—subjects that are essential to surviving as a photographer today.

Although not all Hallmark graduates decide to actually pursue a career in photography immediately after graduation, better than 80 percent of the graduates find successful employment, the majority working for small studios or becoming self-employed. The faculty and staff are experienced working professionals who teach subjects with which they deal on a day-to-day basis.

Courses at Hallmark include:

Traditional Photography
Basic Photography
Retouching I and II
Visual Arts I and II
Advanced Photography

Portrait Photography I and II
Copying
Introduction to Video
Commercial Photography I and II
Portfolio Preparation

Digital Photography
Introduction to Digital Imaging
Advanced Scanning Techniques
Advanced Digital Output
Introduction to Website Design
Digital Workflow: Making Digital Make Sense
    in a Business
Advanced Digital Capture
Advanced Web Design

Business Management
Planning and Analysis Tools
Business Communications
Career Observations I through IV
Site Selection
Current Studio Operations
Business Organization
Plans for Business Control
Color Laboratories
Studio Layout and Design

Marketing
Principles of Professional Photography
Advertising

Salesmanship
Public Relations I and II
Sales Promotion
Marketing Analysis
Pricing
Packaging
Out-of-Studio Displays
Product Development
Selling Plans
Contracts and Proposals
Allied Products

Finance
Record Keeping
Purchasing and Inventory
Financing
Business Law

Personnel
Personality Development
Employee Relations, Compensation, and Motivation
Career Development I, II, and III
Training, Education, and Advancement
Part-Time Employees, Outside Services
Self-Improvement

Degree Programs

There are approximately eight hundred colleges and universities in the United States offering courses that lead to degrees in photography and related fields. Some of these schools are listed in Appendix B.

Ithaca College (ithaca.edu) in Ithaca, New York, is an example of a comprehensive photography program at the bachelor's degree level. Ithaca's Roy H. Park School of Communications offers majors in cinema and photography and in film, photography, and visual arts, among other related programs. An especially attractive element at Ithaca is its program of internships. Recent students have earned professional experience at MTV, Eastman Kodak, CNN, and other leading organizations.

Another example is the Bachelor of Science in Photography offered by Northern Arizona University (nau.edu) in Flagstaff. This degree offers instruction and guidance with a professional perspective in commercial photography and its related fields. The degree is designed to prepare a graduate for a career in commercial photography through a blending of academic and practical experiences. The courses in the major along with the communication core and electives provide an integrated approach to communication.

Two of the best-known schools offering degree programs are the School of Photographic Arts and Sciences at the Rochester Institute of Technology (rit.edu) and Brooks Institute of Photography (brooks.edu).

Rochester Institute of Technology

The School of Photographic Arts and Sciences at the Rochester Institute of Technology (RIT) offers undergraduate two-year (A.A.S.), four-year (B.F.A., B.S.), and graduate-level (M.F.A., M.S.) degrees. All levels of degrees are offered in a variety of photographic specializations. The primary goal of the RIT professional photography curriculum is to prepare the individual student for a career involving photography as a chief means of support. Degrees offered include:

B.F.A. in Professional Photographic Illustration
  (photojournalism)
B.F.A. in Professional Photographic Illustration
  (advertising photography)
B.F.A. in Professional Photographic Illustration (fine art
  photography)
B.S. in Biomedical Photographic Communications
B.S. in Imaging Systems Management (interdisciplinary
  program)
B.S. in Imaging and Photographic Technology
M.F.A. in Imaging Arts, with concentration in fine art
  photography

The current RIT course catalog lists more than 180 courses in the School of Photographic Arts and Sciences. A sample of course titles at this school includes:

Photography I
History and Aesthetics of Photography
Landscape as Photography
Dada and Surrealism
Photography and Critical Theory
Materials and Processes of Photography
Photographic Sensitometry
Technical Photographic Chemistry
Photographic Optics
Color Printing Theory

Color Measurement
Color Photo/Design
Nature Photography
Architectural Photography
Introduction to Digital Image Processing
Electronic Sensitometry
Introduction to Portable Video
Introduction to Multimedia
High-Speed/Time-Lapse
Survey of Nonconventional Imaging

In addition, independent studies and group seminars are arranged throughout the year to explore specialized techniques in photography. Some short workshops and seminars are offered during summer months, and the school offers co-op placements at both local and national levels. Past placements have included companies such as Eastman Kodak, General Electric, National Geographic, Time, Adobe, Apple, IBM, Hewlett Packard, ITEK, NASA, Harley-Davidson, and *Popular Photography* magazine.

Brooks Institute of Photography

Another highly respected, independent photography school is Brooks Institute of Photography in Santa Barbara, California. Brooks offers A.A., B.A., and M.S. degrees, as well as weekend workshops and diploma programs. According to the website, by attending the school, "Students gain the artistic, technical, and business expertise needed to succeed in visual communications. Brooks Institute's programs are designed for anyone who aspires to a career in photography or filmmaking as well as working photographers who seek new skills to advance their careers."

Photographic-major programs offered at Brooks include:

Commercial
Advertising
Digital Imaging
Digital Media
Industrial/Scientific
Motion Picture/Video Production
Portraiture
Visual Journalism
Visual Communications

Canadian Photo Education Programs

Most, but not all, of the college-level photography courses offered in Canada are found in the Province of Ontario in two-year programs at junior colleges, which are called colleges of applied arts and technology. Some offer fields such as multimedia production and film production, which include courses related to photography. These colleges include:

Algonquin College of Applied Arts and Technology
1385 Woodroffe Avenue
Ottawa K2G 1V8
Ontario
algonquin.com

Confederation College of Applied Arts and Technology
1450 Nakina Drive
P.O. Box 398
Thunder Bay P7C 4W1
Ontario
confederationc.on.ca

Fanshawe College of Applied Arts and Technology (3 programs,
    including e-Photo Journalism)
Communication Arts
1460 Oxford Street
P.O. Box 7005
London N5Y 5R6
Ontario
fanshawec.on.ca

Humber College of Applied Arts and Technology (creative
    photography)
205 Humber College Boulevard
Toronto M5T 2T9
Ontario
humber.ca

Loyalist College of Applied Arts and Technology (photojournalism)
Wallbridge-Loyalist Road
P.O. Box 4200
Belleville K8N 5B9
Ontario
loyalistc.on.ca

Sheridan College of Applied Arts and Technology (applied
    photography)
1430 Trafalgar Road
Oakville L6H 2L1
Ontario
sheridanc.on.ca

A Bachelor of Applied Arts in Image Arts–Photography Studies
is offered by:

Ryerson University
350 Victoria Street
Toronto M5B 2K3
Ontario
ryerson.ca

In addition, several Canadian institutions in locations other than the Ontario area offer advanced photography instruction. These include Alberta College of Art and Design, which offers a B.F.A. in Photographic Arts and a Bachelor of Design in Photography:

Alberta College of Art and Design
1407 Fourteenth Avenue NW
Calgary T2N 4R3
Alberta
acad.ab.ca

A bachelor's degree in photography is available through:

University of Victoria
3800 Finnerty Road
Victoria V8P 5C2
British Columbia
uvic.ca

Workshop and Short-Term Programs

In addition to degree and certificate programs, there are outstanding short workshop programs available on almost every facet of photography.

Some schools operate short-term programs that provide concentrated training in photography. For example, the Rocky Mountain School of Photography in Missoula, Montana (rmsp.com), offers an

11-week "Summer Intensive" program that runs from May through mid-August. In 2004 the tuition was $4,495 plus a $200 lab fee.
The courses included:

Advanced Photographic Studies
Basic Photographic Studies
Black and White Darkroom
Black and White Zone System
Business and Marketing
Digital Imaging
Field Trips
Flash Photography
History of Photography
Introduction to Larger Formats
Special Topics
Studio Lighting

Among its other offerings, Rocky Mountain School of Photography also offers a "Digital Intensive" program, a six-week course that runs from mid-August through the end of September. The tuition in 2004 was $4,495 plus a $200 lab fee.
The courses included:

Advanced Photoshop
Color Management
Creative Options
Digital Preparation for Press Printing
Fine Art Printing
Introduction to Adobe Photoshop
Introduction to Digital Imaging
Photography and the Web
The Digital Studio

The "Digital Intensive" program immediately follows the "Summer Intensive" program, and the school gives a $1,000 discount to students who enroll in both. The Rocky Mountain School of Photography offers other programs as well, including field programs held on location at sites such as the coast of Maine, Olympic National Park, and Yosemite. Check out its website for more information.

Scholarships and Financial Aid

The rapid rise in college expenses in recent decades has far outstripped the rise in most other living costs, and the spiral at this time seems endless.

A student going to a public university, if he or she is a resident of the state, will typically spend a total of approximately $7,000 to $10,000 per year. In some cases, the outlay will run substantially higher. Basic yearly charges at private universities average $15,000 to $20,000 or more. Books, clothing, transportation, and other expenses can add another $2,000 to $3,000 to the basic costs. Since the cost of supporting educational institutions is going up yearly, it would be best to write to the colleges or universities you would be interested in attending to get the latest tuition rates and charges for room and board.

Tuition Assistance

Although costs have risen considerably, the College Scholarship Service reports that it is now easier for families of all income levels to qualify for government-subsidized student loans. Most leading banks have details on the low-interest Stafford Loan Program educational loans. Several other loan and grant programs also are available for those demonstrating financial need.

Economic trends have increased the pressure for more scholarships for students, as well as more government aid to colleges and universities. These trends have also contributed to the increase in popularity of two-year community colleges. Students attending these schools typically continue to live at home and keep costs down that way.

Due to the surprising number of financial aid programs and scholarships, along with the increasing opportunities to obtain work while going to school, it is safe to say that serious students can manage some way to work and borrow themselves through almost any course of education they choose to pursue.

Most schools offering photography courses also have qualifications information for applicants on scholarships. These will gladly be explained for the asking.

The Photographic Society of America (PSA) annually awards stipends to provide tuition assistance in the amount of $1,500. The stipends are available to photo career freshmen at both the Brooks Institute of Photography and the Rochester Institute of Technology. Full-time students at either school may apply through the school for these scholarships in the spring of their freshman year. Both a written application and a portfolio of the individual's work are requested. Information is available at the organization's website, psa-photo.org.

Other Scholarships and Grants

Not all scholarships are tied into college tuition. Many states have a Council on the Arts or a similarly named group that offers annual monetary grants for individuals working in various artistic fields, including photography and filmmaking. Check references in your local library to determine the name, or names, of any groups in your state and write for information. You might qualify for a grant, scholarship, or research fellowship.

Photo Contests

Numerous photographic contests are conducted by various organizations each year. Some offer quite respectable cash prizes or equipment. State fairs have contests for many different subjects, including photography. You will never know just how good your own photography is until you enter some prints to be judged by qualified experts.

Internships

Internship programs are offered to a few selected students by:

The International Center of Photography
1114 Avenue of the Americas
New York, NY 10028
icp.org

The International Museum of Photography and Film
George Eastman House
900 East Avenue
Rochester, NY 14607
eastman.org

Several newspapers offer internships in photography. These are usually summer positions for students to fill in for vacationing staff photographers. Inquire about internships at newspapers in your area.

Kodak Scholarships

The Eastman Kodak Company has awarded endowed scholarships to several major photographic colleges and universities. In addition,

Kodak has been awarding one-time scholarships for the value of actual in-state tuition for one academic year (up to a maximum of $2,000 each) to 30 institutions around the United States. These one-time scholarships are awarded to full-time students who have completed one full year of coursework. Students of both two-year associate programs and four-year bachelor's degree programs are eligible.

Reference Materials

Finally, your local library should have copies of reference books for all types of financial assistance, such as *The College Board Scholarship Handbook*. Listed therein are several scholarships, ranging from $100 to $4,000, for various areas of photography. Sources of financial assistance available to college students are described in these reference books:

Blum, Laurie. *Free Money for College*. New York: Checkmark Books, 1999.

The College Board and Joseph A. Russo. *The College Board Scholarship Handbook 2004*. New York: The College Board, 2003.

Edelson, Phyllis, ed. *Foundation Grants to Individuals*. New York: The Foundation Center, 2003.

Leider, Anna J., Robert Leider, and Octameron Associates. *Don't Miss Out: The Ambitious Student's Guide to Financial Aid*. Alexandria, Va.: Octameron Associates, 2003.

National Scholarship Research Service and Daniel J. Cassidy. *The Scholarship Book 2003: The Complete Guide to Private-Sector Scholarships, Fellowships, Grants, and Loans for the Undergraduate*. Upper Saddle River, N.J.: Prentice Hall Press, 2002.

3

GETTING STARTED IN PHOTOGRAPHY

ALMOST EVERYONE LEARNS to use a camera, but most people remain amateurs. Those who take their work to an increasingly higher level form the pool from which professional photographers are drawn.

So how do you know if you have the potential for professional photography? First will come a compelling desire to produce images that attract the attention of others. The intensity of your desire to improve will determine how many photos you take and whether you choose to do your own darkroom work or go straight to digital.

In getting started, consider visiting camera shops and attending amateur photography club meetings in your high school, local community college, or through other community organizations. This will broaden your knowledge of the fundamentals of picture making. If you have managed to invest in a camera of your own—perhaps a good digital camera or a film camera with interchangeable lenses—you are on your way to making better photographs. Traditionally, the next step would be to look for an enlarger, three or four small trays, and a room you can close off to have complete darkness—then you'd be in business. However, now the options are greater. If your clients are likely to be websites and your photography digital, then investing in a good computer with sufficient memory might be all you need.

You should read photography magazines and books and arrange to visit an advanced amateur's setup or a professional photographer's studio. Observing the type and amount of equipment used by them will show you what you are getting into. Only by asking questions will you learn what expenses you will have if you decide to expand your own darkroom facilities and camera equipment. After your visits to camera stores, an amateur's darkroom, or to a professional photographer's studio, as well as talking to your counselor in school—provided you are still a student—you should know how strong your desire is to advance in the photography field.

Let us assume you now own a good camera (digital, 35mm, or 120 size), have read some books, have a darkroom setup of your own, have exposed some films and made prints, and have visited camera stores and a professional photography studio. The next step would be to think of finding part-time work helping a professional photographer in any capacity available.

Experience in School

Most high schools have a darkroom with some equipment, a student newspaper, a camera club, or a yearbook. Let it be known that you would like to be a staff member of one of the student publications and join the camera club. Architects and school boards across the country have incorporated darkrooms and facilities in school buildings because photography has become so important to communications programs. Also, high school camera clubs have proven to be valuable to the schools in gaining additional publicity and recognition in local newspapers, besides providing greater pictorial coverage for yearbooks and student newspapers.

A fine organization with an impressive photography program and national photography contest, active in many rural high schools, is the 4-H Clubs of America (4-H.org). Information on this organization's photography program may be obtained by contacting your local high school principal, the office of your county Cooperative Extension Service, your state department of agriculture, or by writing directly to the 4-H Program Extension service.

If you are going to be active in your camera club, 4-H project, the yearbook, or on the student newspaper staff, don't overlook the chance of making some outside money to pay the costs of your equipment and materials. This can be done by making the acquaintance of your neighborhood newspaper editor to see if you can furnish occasional photographs of school activities for use in the newspaper. Find out the technical preferences and preferred format. Selling extra prints from your negatives to students and their parents is another income-producing idea that will help you increase and improve your photographic equipment and knowledge.

When you start showing some monetary return on your photography investment, you will have a new and different outlook on photography as a valuable lifetime hobby or profession. This also could be the beginning of your career in the business world. Thousands of high school graduates have gone into trade schools and colleges with high school photography experience and earned their tuition, cost of books, and room and board by selling photographs on campus or working as a technician or photographer with student publications. In addition, remember that you could still represent your college, neighborhood, or weekly or daily newspaper as a campus photographer. Remember, too, that the hometown newspaper editor could use that occasional photograph of the community's students receiving recognition while away at college.

An example of being successful in working one's way through college by selling photographs is Victor Keppler. By taking pictures and selling them wherever he could, Mr. Keppler was able to work his way through high school, college, and law school. He did so well financially and enjoyed photography so much that he continued to become one of America's most successful professional photographers. The history of photography lists many other big names who worked their way to the top with photography while learning all they possibly could about the profession.

You would not need to wait until you have gone to college or received a degree in photography to start making a name for yourself. High school is a good time to start, even though many have started gaining recognition after graduating from college and even after retirement from other professions.

Even though photography as a hobby or as a profession can be rewarding from a monetary standpoint, we would not recommend going into the profession purely for the sake of making money. Be sure that photography is the one occupation that will give you the most pleasure and personal satisfaction. If there is another profession that comes to mind that would give you more enjoyment, then pursue it, and use photography as a hobby or sideline.

Competitions

In high school you should start making exhibition prints or slides for camera club exhibits and entering competitions such as the annual Picture of the Year competition sponsored by the National Scholastic Press Association. Entries are judged in four categories— news, features, sports, and fine arts. This competition is excellent for rating your ability compared with other high school photographers throughout the country. If you are unable to get information on this contest through your school, contact:

National Scholastic Press Association
2221 University Avenue SE, Suite 121
Minneapolis, MN 55414
studentpress.org

Other competitions are sponsored by Boy and Girl Scouts of America and the YMCA. Besides the cash and scholarships you get from photo contests, the recognition, publicity, and satisfaction of winning top awards for your creative ability is something that you could never place a monetary value on.

For information on photography opportunities in these organizations, write:

Boy Scouts of America
P.O. Box 152079
Irving, TX 75015
scouting.org

Girl Scouts of the USA
420 Fifth Avenue
New York, NY 10018
girlscouts.org

YMCA of the USA
1015 Eighteenth Street NW
Washington, DC 20036
ywca.org

Several major professional photographic organizations listed below offer reduced-rate student memberships to individuals studying photography on an advanced level. Joining one or more organizations that deal with a specialized area in which you are interested often provides you with mailings, publications, and the opportunity to attend the annual convention as a member. At the convention, you may make contacts that will help you further your career plans or even find employment after graduation.

Advertising Photographers of America, New York
27 West Twentieth Street, Suite 601
New York, NY 10011
http://apany.com

American Society of Media Photographers (ASMP)
150 North Second Street
Philadelphia, PA 19106
asmp.org

Canadian Association of Photographers and Illustrators in
   Communications (CAPIC)
55 Mill Street
The Case Good Building, Suite 302
Toronto M5A 3C4
Ontario
Canada
capic.org

National Press Photographers Association, Inc. (NPPA)
3200 Croasdaile Drive, Suite 306
Durham, NC 27705
nppa.org

Photo Marketing Association International (PMAI)
3000 Picture Place
Jackson, MI 49201
pmai.org

Professional Photographers of America (PPofA)
229 Peachtree Street NE, Suite 2200
International Tower
Atlanta, GA 30303
ppa.org

Professional Photographers of Ontario
2833 Donelly Drive, RR #4
Kemptville K0G 1J0
Ontario
Canada
professionalphotographersofontario.com

Photographing family pets, younger brothers and sisters, and the neighbor's children is the way many professional photographers got their start in making pictures for a living. After photographing children and pets and selling prints to help with the purchasing of more film and equipment, word passes on to relatives and friends, who in turn want more pictures made. As the volume of business increases, so do the facilities for processing, printing, and photographing. The next move usually is into making portraits and photographing weddings. This is probably why many photographers who got their start in this manner often end up owning portrait studios or working with other portrait photographers.

Strategies for Obtaining Employment

Once you have had the experience of working for a camera shop, professional photographer, or in a company photographic department, you have made the first step toward obtaining future employment. It is through these valuable contacts that you learn of other photographers and photographic establishments. Always take advantage of new contacts in the photographic world. Talk with all the photographers you can and ask questions about things you do not understand. Let it be known at your camera club and photographic meetings that you are interested in a job where you can get more photographic experience. In most cases, you stand a better chance of getting the kind of job you want if you know a specific person to contact, rather than simply placing an application through a personnel office. Sometimes, however, the latter is the only way you have to make a contact in distant locations and with large company photographic departments.

Unless you have been fortunate enough to have had the time and facilities in high school or college to make a good assortment of enlargements of diversified subject matter to show a prospective employer, you will have to rely on making a good impression in your interviews. Much will depend on your appearance, speech, eagerness to get the job, and references from former employers and school professors. Here, too, prizes, awards, and recognition gained through photography contests will be most helpful to you. If nothing else, having won awards shows an extra interest in photography. This will be impressive to anyone looking for someone with real interest in advancing in photography.

Your portfolio of photographs should be uniform in size— 8 × 10, 11 × 14, or 16 × 20 inches—and clean and varied in subject matter. A professional folder from some art or office supply store that you use to carry your photographs mounted on mount boards will be professional in appearance. Be sure your prints are spotted carefully. Do not have ragged or crooked borders on your sample prints. Trim the borders off if you must use prints in this condition. In addition, do not put large lettering and your name on the front of your prints.

For appointments with commercial studios and company photographic departments, you should have some views showing products, buildings, equipment, furniture, fashions, automobiles, and groups of people and things. Your work should include close-up, medium-range, and long-distance views. Transparencies should be mounted in transparent vinyl-pocketed sheets for viewing over a light table. If arrangements can be made ahead of time, you may decide to present your images on a computer from a CD or put your 35mm transparencies in a carousel-type projector tray. Whatever you do, select very few examples of your work. Don't overwhelm your interviewer with a large number of photographs. Also, pictures of your little brother and sister are not impressive.

Don't depend on the judgment of your own family and friends for selecting the photographs to show to get a job. Take your portfolio of photographs and slides to some highly respected professional photographer and ask him or her for help and advice. Most recognized photographers will find time to help a young, eager photographer get started.

Attending Conventions

If you possibly can, attend a photographic convention in your community, state, or province to show your samples and seek professional advice. You would not have to stay overnight if costs would be prohibitive and time would be limited. Drive to the convention and back the same day or for one evening. Take your CD, sample photographs, or slides and a list of notes to get opinions. At a convention, you should be able to get several good opinions from name photographers, as well as be able to see displays of professional photographs. Ask other photographers about certain photographs on display and what they think are the outstanding features of some of the photographs hanging in the exhibition. Take your camera along to make exposures of the award-winners and other prints that appeal to you, so that you can take them back home to analyze and study. Just be sure that you use the exposures you make at the convention only for your own knowledge and not for any other purpose.

Whether or not you are a member of the photography group holding the convention will make no difference. Professional photographers are usually all around the hotel or convention hall, and the photographic exhibition is hung where the public can view it. If you are sincere and have a strong enough desire to see and hear a certain name photographer talk, you should have no trouble convincing an officer or board member to allow you to attend a particular program. There are usually student or associate memberships available that would not be too costly.

Bulletin boards for "help wanted" cards are usually on display at most photography conventions. Be sure to check this opportunity for finding employment. Post your name, address, and phone number. Also talk to as many photographic department managers and studio owners as possible.

Knocking on Doors

"Knocking on doors" is a fast way to get acquainted and learn of employment possibilities in photographic departments. Check the Yellow Pages of the phone book for a list of photographic establishments, and if you are a student or graduate, go to the placement bureau of your college or trade school. These are good sources for finding the places to call on for possible employment. Be sure to ask each person with whom you talk if he or she can recommend a company with a job opening.

Being aggressive, persistent, and enthusiastic about seeking employment will be to your advantage. If you have a CD or portfolio of photographs, take them along in case you are asked to show samples. Leave your name, address, and telephone number—typed or written neatly on a plain white card—with the department manager or person interviewing you.

Writing Application Letters

Letter writing should be used as your last resort in getting a photographic job. Naturally, there would be no other way, other than the cost of telephone conversations, or perhaps use of the Internet, to apply for positions in other cities or states where time and expense would rule out direct contact. Writing effective letters of application is a skill in itself. Prepare a letter on plain white or cream paper giving information in separate paragraphs on the type of position wanted, education, experience, professional and community memberships, references, and personal information. Keep the letter simple, neat, and to the point, avoiding the use of "I" as much as possible. Again, seeking advice from someone more expert in letter or résumé writing would be a smart move on your part. Take a draft letter, written to the best of your ability, to someone in your school such as the career resource center or guidance counselor, or a local business, to check and get helpful suggestions for improving its effectiveness. There also are a number of books on résumé and letter writing available at your local library or bookstore.

When you are satisfied that you have prepared the most effective application possible, there are a number of sources available for obtaining a list of places to send the letters. Your best bet for this list is the telephone company office or a large library. Ask your telephone company to let you see telephone directories of the cities in which you think you would like to live and work—then look under "photography" and "photographic establishments" in the Yellow

Pages for places to write. You can also ask your local librarian for reference materials or look online.

Using Advertising to Get Employment

If you wish to place classified advertisements for employment, here are some addresses of publications to write to for costs and deadline dates. Address your inquiries to the advertising department.

American Cinematographer
1782 North Orange Drive
Los Angeles, CA 90028
tehasc.com

Editor and Publisher
770 Broadway
New York, NY 10003
editorandpublisher.com

News Photographer (c/o NPPA)
3200 Croasdaile Drive, Suite 306
Durham, NC 27705
nppa.org

Photo Marketing
3000 Picture Place
Jackson, MI 42901
pmai.org

The Professional Photographer
229 Peachtree Street NE, Suite 2200
International Tower
Atlanta, GA 30303
ppmag.com

The Rangefinder
1313 Lincoln Boulevard
P.O. Box 1703
Santa Monica, CA 90406
rangefinder.com

Studio Photography and Design
445 Broad Hollow Road, Suite 221
Melville, NY 11747
imaging-info.com

These same publications are excellent sources for finding help-wanted advertisements. You could answer some of these ads before spending money on advertising. Also check the help-wanted advertisements in your daily and nearby big city newspapers. One never knows for sure where the best opportunity lies for the future. Be sure to try them all.

In each state there are photography magazines, trade journals, bulletins, and mailing pieces sent regularly to members by state and large city professional photographers' associations. These are close-to-home publications with advertisements for help that receive good response because the publications are quickly and easily read. To find out about them, you would have to contact a company photographer or a studio owner for back issues or request that the next issue be saved for you.

Advantages of a Career in Photography

Photography as a profession can offer immense personal enjoyment and satisfaction. You can use it for the enjoyment of your whole family—while on vacations, in your home, during spare time, in another business, as a hobby, and on your job.

Photography includes some lucrative fields in which a darkroom and studio are not even necessary, such as supplying images for websites and business presentations.

Good public relations and the character of people working in the photographic field are important. As in most other professions, an increasing number of dedicated members in professional photography associations are campaigning to improve the principles of conduct governing individuals and group operations.

Flexibility is another key asset for any photographer. Peter Gowland has reminisced on occasions how he photographed weddings, made passport photos, and took anything he could get while he developed his flourishing, nationally known photography business. A well-known portrait photographer, who built a multimillion-dollar business, got started in photography while working as a streetcar conductor. A freelance commercial photographer roams the world furnishing photographs for travel agencies, airlines, passenger ships, magazines, and advertising agencies. He moved from San Francisco to Hawaii. Any number of success stories could be mentioned to illustrate opportunities in this field.

Photography is a field in which initiative, enthusiasm, creativity, and long hours can be rewarded with professional recognition, tremendous personal satisfaction, and just about any amount of money you want. Laziness, indifference, negative attitudes, sloppiness, and looking for an easy way out are the characteristics that will surely lead to failure in photography.

Other chapters in this book cover the varied fields of specialization, general photography opportunities, and how well each pays. Read these chapters, check your local library for photo publications, and talk with as many photographers as you can manage to meet, then make up your mind whether to go all the way in choosing photography as a lifetime profession. If you do decide that photography is for you, and you have most of the qualities mentioned, you will never regret your decision.

Earning Potential

How much a photographer earns, in terms of dollars and cents, is the most difficult question to answer in this book. It is like answering the question: how much is creativity worth? Unfortunately, estimates of salaries and wages in the photographic field vary considerably and these figures are based on a variety of factors, including your level of talent and how much time and effort you put into getting the word out about your work.

The following information has been obtained from a variety of reliable references. Most dollar amounts are averages, so actual low- and high-end salaries are much different than the dollars mentioned. Salaries also will vary by geographic region and be affected by changes in the economy in general. However, the information here will serve as a point of reference and will give you an idea of the fluctuations in earnings in photography.

Apprentice beginners generally earn minimum wage while they get started as all-around helpers in portrait, commercial, or similar studios, depending on the individual's qualifications and the size of the firm or city. If you get the opportunity to work as an apprentice under a photographer who has a good reputation, it would be wise to seriously consider taking the job primarily for the experience and guidance. Some students will accept this type of employment for part-time work while continuing their formal education. Photo lab technicians doing processing and printing also typically earn minimum wage or a little over. Opportunities for advancement vary, with advancement more likely in a store that specializes in photography and is willing to train staff.

After a few years of practical on-the-job experience, industrial photographers employed by corporations would have an advantage over employees of private studios because there are usually better fringe benefits and more frequent reviews for salary increases.

Large firms with photographic studios tend to pay better than commercial or portrait studios. A person with a two-year or four-year degree in photography will have a better chance of obtaining a position than a person with similar experience and no degree.

Portrait studios tend to be owned and managed by one person but frequently have other family members working there. Sometimes there are some part-time or full-time additional photographers to help out in busy seasons.

Independent photographers and freelancers have the broadest range of incomes. The majority of them probably earn only enough to make a modest living. But they stay in business because they enjoy the freedom of being their own bosses and being able to say yes or no to any assignment. There are a number of photographers who have made a name for themselves and can command very high fees for any assignment they choose to accept.

Magazine Photographs

Attempting to provide an approximation of the value of a photograph published in a magazine is difficult since there are so many variances. Some publications receive only small local distribution, others are regional, and the most widely circulated publications receive national distribution. The total circulation of a magazine is one of the primary criteria for establishing a print price, as is the size and location of the photograph used in print. Inside editorial usage seldom pays much, while any advertising usage of a picture will normally command top-dollar return for the photographer.

A small reproduction of a picture used to illustrate a story or article will naturally receive far less attention—and payment—than an eye-catching photo used on the cover. Cover photos rightfully receive the most pay, especially those used on newsstand publications, which depend on attracting the attention of shoppers and enticing them to purchase that issue of the magazine. An exclusive, unique, or rare photograph, especially one of a news event or some unusual happening that nobody else was able to photograph, will command a much higher price than a merely attractive or outstanding photo that anybody could have the opportunity to make. In fact, one photographer made thousands of dollars for his dramatic photographs of the Mount St. Helens volcanic eruption—but he almost lost his life in the process of making those pictures!

Large-circulation (or distribution) magazines pay the most, while controlled, low-circulation magazines that number their readers at 50,000 or fewer will pay considerably less for a similar photo.

One-time use rights are normally stipulated with the sale of any photo, so the picture is merely "leased" for this one use only. In actuality, one photo can be resold many times for use in different publications if it is unusual or commands attention. Thus, the income derived from rare or especially interesting pictures can continue for years. Conversely, sometimes a picture is sold outright, with all rights going to the buyer, who gains full control over its use. For this type of sale, a higher payment should be contracted since the photographer no longer owns the picture after the sale. There are other types of image rights that apply to photographs and their publication, but we will not go into detail about them.

A good source of information about markets for photographs is *Photographer's Market*, edited by Donna Poehner (Cincinnati, Oh.: Writer's Digest Books, 2003).

Art Photography

Photographs are often recognized as a form of art by museums, corporations, banks, galleries, and individual collectors. Along with this recognition come corresponding prices commanded for outstanding photographs by well-known photographers. For example, one self-portrait of photographer Robert Mapplethorpe, who died of AIDS in 1989, sold for close to $40,000. Recent photography sales at auction houses such as Sotheby's and Christie's, and at some prominent New York City galleries, have resulted in sales of photographs much in excess of their estimated value. Some photos even sold for up to triple the estimates, with some top-quality prints made by Alfred Stieglitz during his lifetime selling in a group of 21 for a record $396,000. A self-portrait of Paul Outerbridge sold for $99,000.

Quality photographs made by early photographers, especially those from a limited edition and signed, can be good investments. This does not imply that every photograph could potentially have such a high value, but outstanding examples of recognized master photographers are finally receiving the recognition and respect deserved by pioneers of the medium. Current sales trends show that creative, reliable photographers who can consistently produce top-quality results under a wide variety of circumstances can make considerable money.

4

COMMERCIAL PHOTOGRAPHY

SEPARATING THE TYPE of subjects or activities done by the commercial, portrait, or industrial photographer is difficult because there is a natural overlapping of each category. Even the equipment used can be similar, if not identical. In general, the commercial photographer photographs inanimate objects or things; the portrait photographer is more involved with people. Many smaller studios have only one or two photographers who wear many hats and produce quality images of both objects and people for their clients.

Commercial photographers produce images of many subjects. Typical subjects would be:

Construction and
  architecture
Real estate
Sales meetings
Conventions
Trade shows
Golf tournaments

Sailing, automobile, and
  other races
Banquets
Store and mall displays
Fashion and clothing
Manufactured items

These photographs might be used for publicity brochures or ads, websites, company publications, catalogs, business and trade publications, display or wall decor, or postcards. The photographs record events or things for advertising, sales and promotional activities, and public relations for the client.

The commercial photographer is, in effect, a salesperson through photographs. Since he or she will be called upon to photograph a variety of subjects, the photographer must be versatile, quick to understand how the product works in order to photograph it intelligently, and able to exercise ingenuity. Learning all about a client's products and operation is important to hold an account for a long period of time. With this knowledge, the photographer can make photographs that will do a better job of selling the customer's products. The ability to tell the company's story photographically better than any other photographer is a priceless talent and one that will help retain clients and bring increased business.

Commercial photography, however, is not the field for an up-and-coming photographer who wishes to take the time to do art photography. Commercial photography requires working under pressure. Sometimes it means being on call day and night, Sundays, and even holidays. Often the jobs the commercial photographer undertakes have a tight schedule and a rigid deadline.

Time is of the essence in commercial photography, and one of the photographer's most valuable commodities is fast service. The photographer must be ready to go at a moment's notice. It is not unusual for the photographer to answer the phone, receive a request from a customer, and be on the way to the assignment in a few minutes. Often photographers take the assignment in the afternoon and deliver the finished prints early the next morning. Because time is such a vital factor in commercial photography, some photographers maintain a complete set of equipment in their cars, ready to go at all times. Failure to give speedy and dependable service has probably been responsible for more lost business than any other cause in commercial photography.

Commercial photographers range from the small-town businessperson who also does some portraits to the celebrated big-city illustrator who receives several thousand dollars for a single photograph. Although the latter gets high fees, the expenses are considerable. The photographer needs a good deal of working space, which means taking on the cost of renting or leasing a large studio; an extensive assortment of equipment; and complete set-building facilities, to mention but a few examples. Because the pictures one is assigned to make are often used in costly advertisements, clients are willing to pay the high fee of the prominent photographer, confident that he or she will produce an effective photograph. They cannot afford to take risks by hiring a photographer of unknown skills with the high cost of the advertising space, deadlines, model fees, and other expenses. Much depends on the effectiveness, that is, on the selling power, of the picture.

Obviously, it takes a long time to reach the level of the large commercial studios, most of which are located in large cities, where important accounts have offices.

The majority of commercial studios do a general business— anything that comes along. As indicated previously, a commercial photographer may be called upon to photograph anything from banquets to window displays, from glassware to fashion, from passport photos to publicity pictures for magazines and newspapers. The tendency, however, is to specialize in one field.

Some commercial photography studios specialize in architectural photography. Photography for catalogs is yet another popular specialization. Specialization is usually highly individualized. The photographer-owner does most of the work, with the help of assistants. There are also career opportunities in commercial photography studios for stylists—those who are responsible for details such as selecting props, dressing the set, and putting finishing touches on models' clothing—and for sales representatives and business managers. Of course, often many laboratory technicians are needed.

Some of the best creative photography is being done in the fashion field, which calls for a combination of the artist and fashion expert, as well as a sharp eye for significant detail and the ability to portray the fashion product attractively.

Advantages and Disadvantages

In the event the commercial photographer plans to go into business for her- or himself, it would be wise to consider some of the disadvantages of this area of photography. There are long hours, last-minute rush assignments, deadline pressures, large investments in equipment, and the risks that any person takes when going into a business. However, some of these disadvantages do not exist if the photographer is an employee of a large commercial studio.

On the other hand, there are compensations and much personal satisfaction in this type of photography. It takes a particular kind of business acumen to operate a successful commercial photography studio. There is the challenge of dealing directly with other successful businesspeople who come to you with various assignments. The work is challenging and diverse, because no two jobs are alike. A chance to travel and the opportunity to learn firsthand about many different types of businesses and products are some other advantages of commercial photography.

The financial return for a commercial photography business can be very lucrative, especially if it is clear that your images have helped to increase demand for your clients' products. Usually, eye-appealing photographs that do a good job of selling are the results of one or more alert photographers in an organization. If one account shows a steady business improvement—through the effectiveness of good photographs—it is more than likely that the same will prove true with all the other accounts. In this way your photographic business will show a steady growth, with an increasing number of new accounts or product lines. The goal is to develop a style of photography that makes companies and agencies come to you for outstanding photographs.

Illustrative or Advertising Photography

Selling or "telling the story" of a company's product for use in advertisements, newspapers, magazines, and for some TV commercials is the job of the illustrative photographer. Going through the pages of almost any national magazine, you should be immediately aware of the high quality of the many ads. It is the photograph's purpose in such an ad to influence the consumer visually to purchase the item, and the success or failure of the ad is reflected in that company's sales figures. The advertiser usually spends an enormous sum of money for these ads, and illustrative photography is a very highly competitive field requiring the latest approaches and techniques in photography. Creativity, however, is the main ingredient added by the photographer that can help build a business and reputation in this particular classification of photography. He or she will work with other talented individuals, such as artists, advertising managers, and art directors. Because they are creative thinkers, illustrative photographers will find working with people who are constantly thinking up new ideas to be interesting and exciting.

The key to illustrative photography is creativity, so there is no single approach the photographer can take to ensure success. Very often the illustrative photographer will work from an artist's sketch of what is to be portrayed in a photograph. Or, he or she will be expected to interpret some idea or concept as an eye-catching sales illustration. At other times, the ideas for photographs may have to be researched by reading and looking at illustrations in libraries, museums, or art galleries. An interior decorator, food economist, or other highly specialized person or technical adviser from another field may have to be consulted in completing the photography setup.

The illustrator often is paid to produce an illustration completely different from anything used before and that bears no resemblance to the competitor's sales presentation or advertisements. Sometimes the model hired plays such an important part in the illustration that many days are spent searching for just the right kind of model to bring the client's concept to life. Going through modeling agency files can be quite time-consuming, especially if you are trying to find a fresh new face never seen before in other advertisements.

Getting the proper backgrounds and settings for certain products to be photographed can also be difficult and the costs considerable. Sometimes the photo illustrator must travel with props and a staff of assistants to complete the job. The matter of a few hundred dollars' expense one way or the other is not important to an agency that is seeking an eye-catching ad to run in *Time, Newsweek, National Geographic, Reader's Digest, The Smithsonian,* or some other national publication. In these publications a full-page advertisement or a two-page spread can cost thousands of dollars to run in a single issue.

Some photo illustrators also have had great success breaking into TV commercial production—which can be an even more lucrative and fast-paced field.

Meetings and Conventions

In convention cities and resort areas, some studios have developed a specialized field of photography. They photograph convention or meeting participants in small and large groups, in formal and informal "at work" situations. Now, with the decentralization of meeting facilities, nearly every hotel can accommodate meetings of organizations and companies. In addition to group photographs, the enterprising photographer will take pictures of workshops, awards presentations, new officer installations, and trade show exhibition booths.

Another profitable business can be built upon the growing need for audiovisual presentations, from a simple slide show to a multimedia production. Many modern hotels are designed with built-in audiovisual facilities, including arrangements for closed-circuit television programming. Along with the growing need for audiovisual programming will develop a body of experienced audiovisual producers, scriptwriters, programmers, and technicians. The growing need for visual material on websites holds similar potential. That said, the person considering audiovisual or website production as a career should be prepared to meet talented competition.

Equipment

Equipment requirements for a commercial photographer can vary considerably from those of photographers engaged solely in portraiture. The commercial photographer will be required to photograph anything from a photomicrographic specimen to the biggest building in the city from a helicopter. Thus, the commercial photographer may need a much greater initial financial outlay than the portrait or industrial photographer.

To have a complete studio, $50,000 to more than $100,000 could be needed. The industrial photographer working for a company would have equipment furnished that is suited to the specific fields covered. The commercial photographer would have to own a car or even a station wagon, van, or truck. In all likelihood, this vehicle would be loaded with a good deal of equipment.

The commercial photographer needs a varied selection of cameras and lenses ready to go at a moment's notice. Digital cameras and film cameras in the 8 × 10, 4 × 5, 2¼ × 2¼, and 35mm sizes all have uses on different jobs, along with an assortment of lenses suitable for each of them.

Commercial photographers rely on electronic flash for the variety of work they are expected to perform. Studio electronic flashes are not very portable; therefore, small portable electronic flashes are frequently used. Incandescent and quartz, as continuous light sources, also will be of great use for catalogs, magazines, and fashion publicity and advertising. Broad, even, diffused light from light banks and other soft light sources is popular today. You must educate yourself on unusual lighting sources so you will be prepared to handle any type of assignment.

A ground-floor or downtown location for a commercial studio would not be as important to the commercial photographer as it might be to the portrait photographer, who caters to a certain number of walk-in customers. However, the commercial photographer who has accounts with companies that manufacture large products, such as appliances, furniture, or automobiles, would need a large, ground-floor location with high ceilings and a side entrance for moving in these large products for photographing.

Darkroom/Laboratory

A commercial photographer should have darkroom equipment in the studio for fast service because the typical commercial customer cannot wait for work to be farmed out to a lab. However, if at the start of your business venture you do not wish to process your own film and enlarge your own prints, you may want to contact one of the professional processing labs in your area and establish a good working rapport with the staff there. You can handle rush jobs even without your own darkroom if you have good connections at the lab.

If you do plan to furnish your own processing and finishing, then equipment such as washers, dryers, enlargers, and contact printers will be essential to give fast delivery of prints to your customers. Automatic processors for film and prints will be a must.

Freelance Photography

Freelance photographers work on their own instead of serving as employees of a business or nonprofit organization. Typically they work for a variety of clients.

Freelancers establish a point of operation where mail and phone calls may be collected and acknowledged wherever they may be working. In many cases, home is their base of operation, including for correspondence and record keeping. Having voice mail and e-mail are critical.

Most freelancers are on the go most of the time—that is, if they are in the top income bracket and their work and names have become prominent enough to make businesses, agencies, photo editors, and syndicates want their photographic services.

Some freelance photographers have their own darkrooms and spend time at the home base doing their own processing and printing, but most arrange with custom laboratories to handle these processes. So even while the photographer is away on another assignment, film can be sent in with instructions to be processed, contact-printed, and delivered to the client. The client studies the contact sheets and indicates how the picture is to be cropped in the enlargement for the intended picture story or advertising layout.

Equipment needed by freelancers who cover assignments anywhere in the United States and out of the country can amount to a sizable investment, although they have to travel with the least possible amount of weight while on the road. Two or three 35mm camera bodies with wide-angle, normal, and long focal length lenses, a 4 × 5 view camera with assorted lenses, as well as a 120 size camera are a must to be prepared to handle a greater percentage of the jobs. Electronic flash equipment also is necessary. If the end product is to be used on a website or PowerPoint presentation, digital cameras may be the equipment of choice. There are many sources listing photo markets in which you may want to include your availability to do assignments. These same sources also can be consulted to sell your stock photos. Some time spent online or at a library making a list of the current market publications and companies that purchase outside photography will be profitable.

One of the better sources of photography sales possibilities is *Working Press of the Nation*, volume 2. It is published by Magazines and Internal Publications (New Providence, N.J.: R. R. Bowker, 2000; bowker.com). This publication includes a freelance guide to more than four thousand of the nation's leading house magazines, listing magazine titles, editors, company names, and addresses, as well as photographic subjects and stock photography agencies.

Another book of interest to the beginner in freelance or stock photography sales is *Photographer's Market*, edited by Donna Poehner (Cincinnati, Oh.: Writer's Digest Books, 2003; writers digest.com). This book is updated each year and has comprehensive listings of the photographic needs in a variety of categories and markets.

Making contacts with the art directors and photo editors of advertising agencies, photo syndicates, newspapers, and magazines is a move in the right direction. After the freelance photographer has established several accounts, he or she can become selective or specialize in a specific type of photography.

Stock Images

Stock picture agencies are always looking for fresh sources of quality photos. However, this is not a "get rich quick" type of photography. Unless you have a quite unusual and visually different photograph that will sell immediately, you should be prepared to furnish several hundred photographs or slides and possibly wait a year or more for any sales to develop. It is, however, a good source of extra income from photography and should be seriously considered by many individuals.

There are several hundred stock agencies all over the United States and Canada. Most handle color and black-and-white pictures of a wide variety of photographic subjects including people, business, scenic, architecture, and cities, while others specialize in topics such as sports, nature, agriculture, glamour, food, news, or history. Several agencies you might want to contact are:

Comstock
244 Sheffield Street
Mountainside, NJ 07092
comstock.com

Getty Images
530 West Twenty-Fifth Street
New York, NY 10001
http://creative.gettyimages.com

PhotoResearchers
60 East Fifty-Sixth Street
New York, NY 10022
photoresearchers.com

Superstock
7660 Centurion Parkway
Jacksonville, FL 32256
superstock.com

Aerial Photography

Some photographers and companies specialize almost exclusively in
the science of photogrammetry—aerial photography—and there
are enough of these companies to warrant the organization of an
association known as the American Society of Photogrammetry and
Remote Sensing (asprs.org). This society sponsors annual conventions and seminars for studying and advancing the work of aerial
photography. Special planes, with cameras installed into the planes'
bottoms, make up a vital part of their expensive and specialized
equipment. The planes are used for mapping and surveying operations throughout the United States and in foreign countries.

The general photography studios found in both small towns and
cities make many aerials. Rented airplanes, planes belonging to
friends, and all kinds of cameras are used in doing the photography. Where aerial cameras like those used in the different branches
of the armed forces are not available, any format handheld camera,
dependent upon the subject matter and quality required by the
client, can make acceptable aerial photographs.

Most of the large-scale photogrammetry work is done for
county, state, and federal governments, as well as for companies
holding large acreages of land and for foreign governments. Pho-

tographs of most state land are on file for use in determining where new charts of highways, pipelines, and rivers will be done. Also, the heights of mountains and depths of valleys and canyons are studied and measured from these aerial photographs. Pollution of rivers and lakes as well as the effects of fires and diseases of forests and crops can be detected through the use of aerial photographs.

Aerial photographs also are used for planning large-scale projects such as the locating of airport sites, railroad systems, power lines, and so on. Other projects involve surveying crop conditions and timberland and recording changes in rivers, shorelines, and mountains where erosion is at work. Still other air-view subject matter includes factories, homes, country clubs, housing projects, and shopping centers. Likely markets for such pictures are the owners of the properties, real estate agents, local officials, colleges, yacht clubs, airports, and newspapers.

Aerial photography is a specialization in which photographers can earn a regular living. Aside from jobs with airlines, employment opportunities can be found in government work and on the staffs of large aerial survey companies. Interpreting photographs of the earth's resources taken from space is a field for future photographers with scientific training and backgrounds.

Lyndon B. Johnson once said, "If we had no justification other than the photography, it would be worth ten times more than the $35 to $40 billion the United States has spent to date on its space program." Many Americans would agree with him.

Some excellent thoughts about aerial photography appeared in *The Professional Photographer* magazine. Harper Leiper, past president of the Professional Photographers of America, wrote:

> There is money to be made in aerial photography but you cannot make it on aerial photography alone. You've got to be doing several things and have income from all of them.

It takes time to build a file of stock aerials. But if you have a good system, they are moneymakers. Our stock file is about 7,000 11 × 14 prints. They account for about a third of our gross now. It's the easiest profit you'll ever make. We have a big map indexed to the file, and the customer just comes in and looks up the area on which he wants an aerial. We charge more for older prints, in increments of ten years.

If a customer purchases an aerial from our stock file and wants more copies of it, he doesn't have to pay the basic fee over again. He can get as many as he wants at our regular reprint rates. Many times they do request 25 to 50 copies.

Every three years I do a City Strip to make a record of the populated areas of Houston. I go to 10,000 feet in a fixed-wing aircraft and, using a handheld camera, shooting at about an 80° angle along a predetermined path, I strip the town at 100 mph. I make an exposure every 30 seconds, and I find that these overlap enough to give me a complete picture of the city.

5

Portrait Photography

A GOOD BEGINNING point for many photographers is outdoor portrait photography because all that is required is a camera, film, and a willing subject. The typical subject of most amateurs' cameras is a family member, friend, pet, or neighborhood child. Naturally, your subjects—except the pet—want to see the finished pictures. If they like them, they will want extra prints to keep. The photographer often is also anxious to see what the photographs look like enlarged. If the subjects can afford it, they may contribute to the cost of film and printing. Thus, a budding business is born. The next major question is: can you continue doing this and produce a regular income?

What to charge for photography is often one of the most difficult decisions to make in the profession. In the beginning it is just a guess, and—believe it or not—some photographers go through a lifetime in the business without being sure they have been fair with their prices. A great number of studios are operated with the photographer's spouse and the assistance of other members of the family. They sometimes work long hours for little or no pay.

As the demand increases for photographs from amateurs, their interest in learning more about the profession increases. Reading more magazines and books, visiting other photographers, and joining photography associations helps in making the decision to go into the business full-time.

At this point, it is wise to think twice and get further counsel on what to do. The important thing to give thought to is whether you have enough training and skill to make sufficient progress in the portraiture field or whether you should first get additional training through workshops, short courses, or as a student in a photography school.

Another consideration is to weigh the advantages of working for an established studio for three or four years to learn the techniques of the business. Most of the older, well-known photographers got their start by serving as assistants or apprentices in studios. Today making the choice is a bit more involved, with so many short courses in every field of photography. In addition, there are good academic courses in high schools, community colleges, and universities, as well as in trade and correspondence schools. Then, too, there is more specialization today than ever before and many new advances because of improved materials and equipment. Technical advances and increasing interest in fine color portraiture will make for continued growth and expansion in this field.

Advantages and Disadvantages

The field of portrait photography can be particularly appealing for several reasons. One plus is the control the photographer has over the use of his or her time. This is probably the only photographic field in which this advantage can be controlled to any great extent. Portrait photographers can schedule sittings for a time convenient to themselves. They can even refer sittings to another studio. A commercial or freelance photographer would have to take the chance of losing an account of many years' standing, running into thousands of dollars, if he or she were not available to do a certain job at a certain time, day or night. Industrial photographers and others working on a salary could not take off any time they wanted to because they would not have any control over the policy concerning their working hours and vacations.

A portrait studio's financial success cannot be judged by its decor or by the number of employees. Nor should it be belittled if it is a family business. It is quite possible that a family-run business with little overhead could be much more profitable than a more elaborate operation with a studio with a large number of employees and a higher gross income.

Despite the philosophy that if you don't keep pace with progress you will fall behind, there are many small, happily established businesses that prefer avoiding additional work and responsibility and make no effort to grow bigger. On the other hand, there are those who do everything in their power to become large businesses and outdo their competitors. In many cases, growth is necessary to keep contracts and maintain an established business. Computerization has become a necessity today with the large portrait studios that sign contracts for photographing senior classes and undergraduates in a large number of schools. Some studios have become such large operations that traveling studios built into trailers are being used to photograph students in several states.

It is possible to build a portrait business into almost any type of business you want, small or large, with growth potential. But remember, too, that a proportionate share of failures and lean years go along with something that has as many pleasures as operating one's own business.

Studio Location

If you have decided to go into this type of photography, after getting experience in a good portrait studio for three or four years or completing a photography program, your next big decision will be that of where to locate your establishment.

Most successful portrait studios are located near potential customers, and those are tremendously varied. Many studios depend largely on getting a good part of the yearly senior portraits from the community's high schools. After doing the senior class portraits in a school, there is a tendency to add another school and then another as the years go on. In this case, then, finding a location for your business near a large school might help you get off to a good start.

Besides adult portraits and high school senior portraits, baby portraits and wedding photography are important segments of a successful portrait studio. Some studios specialize in portraiture of children by orienting all their promotion, decoration, equipment, and presentation in this direction. In the past few years, there has been an increase in the photographing of family groups, pets, and children in the home atmosphere or outdoors in environmental settings. Large dye transfer and other color print finishes, sold in expensive, museum-type frames, have been responsible for building an increasing number of portrait studio businesses into more than $100,000 endeavors.

Initially, you will have to decide whether you want to start working from your home, build a studio, or lease a building. Location of your business and studio should be of prime consideration. It should be located relatively close to a busy shopping area with ample parking nearby so that it is accessible to walk-in customers. Your building should be large enough to have a pleasant reception area and adequate studio space for both individual and group portraits.

Seek the best location available that will be within your estimated operating budget. You should have a good idea of what this should be after talking with other professional photographers and your banker. Also confirm that local zoning ordinances allow a photography studio at the location you select.

Although you may start by renting a space, it would be advisable to keep in mind that you may someday, after building a successful photography business, want to own the location for your business. Parking, a good display window, and a place for a sign are other necessities to make a speedier beginning in business. As your business grows, parking space will become more and more important. Take into consideration, also, that the farther you are from a main street or downtown shopping area, the more you will have to spend on advertising and promotion to keep your name and location constantly in the mind of the buying public.

It will be worth your time to check on the potential growth of the area in which you expect to start, as well as the tax history of the community. Leasing with an option to buy after two or three years is something else to consider. The general appearance and layout of the building you use, along with the adjoining properties, should be appealing to customers. A visit with real estate agents to discuss what you are looking for would prove helpful in gaining valuable knowledge before making a final decision.

Your ability and willingness to learn and to work long, hard hours to get a business going are crucial no matter where you are located. An artistic nature and the ability to produce high-quality photographs, which will win awards in competition with other professional photographers, will attract an increasing number of customers to your business, even though your location may not be as convenient as you would like.

Business Competition

All successful people and businesses face competition. This should be met with an open mind and a favorable attitude. Competition is not limited to others in the portrait photography business. It can be the jeweler, drugstore, gift shop, or appliance store down the street. Each family has just so much money to spend after paying for food, clothing, and housing. Every other business is after the same extra dollars that will be spent for luxuries. To be successful in the portrait field, it is necessary to promote, sell, publicize, advertise, and present your photographs. Making the buying public conscious of your studio and desirous of owning what you have to sell is what will make the real difference in the amount of sales you total up at the end of the year.

Other kinds of marketing techniques you will have to be prepared for are price-cutting, premium offers, contests, telephone solicitation, door-to-door sales, and gimmicks of all kinds by competitors to attract portrait photography customers to their studios.

Fortunately, there seem to be fewer "fly-by-nighters" today than in years past. Larger, automated businesses are doing most of the volume of portrait business in this country today.

In response to increased competition, a portrait studio in Alabama operates a wedding shop adjacent to the studio. Wedding dresses, bridesmaids' dresses, and renting of tuxedos are featured, along with a catering service and gowns for mothers of the bride and groom. Special discounts are given to the bride on her wedding pictures with the purchase of her dress. The addition of a wedding shop has substantially increased the studio's wedding photography business.

Equipment

Most portrait studios use 120-roll film cameras with a medium telephoto lens (about 180mm) to photograph individuals. Of course, shorter focal length lenses also will be needed for photographing couples or groups. Outdoor, environmental photography is very popular today for high school seniors, family groups, and wedding parties. Medium-format, 120-roll film cameras also are used for this type of portraiture outside the studio. More compact and portable 35mm cameras are seldom used for professional portraiture. This is because the 24 × 36mm (35mm film) negative is too small for retouching easily. The 120-film cameras produce an image three to five times larger. It is not only easier to retouch, but also can be enlarged to produce much bigger wall display prints.

A wheeled monopod studio stand for inside work and a sturdy tripod for outdoors are essential for producing top-quality images with the larger, heavier, medium-format cameras. Newer models of these cameras offer optional automatic exposure and motorized film advance features. This automation gives the photographer more time to devote to capturing memorable poses of the subjects.

Lighting

Portrait studio lighting is primarily electronic flash for photographing people of all ages. The bright but extremely short-duration light is excellent for capturing the subject, yet it remains cool. Years ago, continuous light sources, such as tungsten or quartz lamps, were more common. But the portrait subject often became uncomfortable under the hot lighting.

Studio electronic flash units are AC-powered and are bulky. Often they are on wheeled stands that telescope for height adjustment. Also available are overhead rail lighting systems that suspend the light heads from the ceiling. This minimizes the clutter of stands and cords often found in portrait studios. Portrait lights tend to have large reflectors, 12 to 16 inches in diameter. They have movable barn doors and diffusion screens for simple adjustment of the quality of light produced. Each light has its own incandescent modeling light, which makes it simple to position the lights to produce the exact intensities and shadows desired for each individual's unique facial features. The intensity of the modeling lights varies to correspond with the intensity of the flash itself. A minimum of four modeling lights, two floodlights, and two spotlights are needed for quality portraiture.

A soft, complimentary type of studio light frequently used for photographing women is the umbrella light. Most any studio light can be easily adapted to accept an umbrella. Other helpful studio accessories include adjustable-height posing tables, reflectors, and vignetting diffusers to place in front of the lens.

For candid coverage of weddings, bar mitzvahs, and other occasions, more portable cameras and lighting equipment are necessary. Small 35mm equipment is commonly used for these events since this type of camera is far more portable. Compact, powerful electronic flash units can be used on either automatic or manual to adequately light most events. For large groups, several additional flash units, with an electric-eye slave that syncs them with the camera flash, can be an asset in obtaining proper lighting.

Portable flash units are sometimes used for environmental portraiture. More often, white cardboard or fold-up cloth reflectors or umbrellas are carried to provide the additional fill light required in some outdoor situations. Sometimes black umbrellas are used to shade and produce more flattering diffused lighting.

Whether working indoors with artificial lighting or outdoors with natural light, the portrait photographer must always control the lighting so the subjects will look their best. Most individuals do not have their portrait made very often, so it is the photographer's responsibility to produce the best quality possible.

Processing

Although most portrait studios have a rudimentary darkroom on their premises, it frequently is equipped only for basic black-and-white processing and printing. Most portraits, other than press release views, are made on color negative film, and the resulting prints are color enlargements.

Most smaller-volume studios do not produce enough portraits, or have a large enough staff of employees, to justify doing their own color film and print processing in-house. Custom color processing labs are found everywhere today and often offer pickup and delivery service to studios within a nominal driving distance. Even when using mail, or UPS service, round-trip to a color lab usually only takes about a week. So the added costs and skills necessary to install and operate a color-processing lab are impractical. The advent of digital photography promises significant change in this area. Production of photos through the use of computers and color printers is increasingly common.

Smaller portrait studios today find that they must be able to do more than produce quality studio portraits to survive. Large-volume portrait studios operating out of mass merchandising stores provide tough competition on pricing. Independent studios must diversify and offer additional services to keep busy. Environmental portraiture, copy and restoration of old photographs, and framing are several common sidelines that can bring in additional business.

Many skills, in addition to being able to adjust the lights and expose film correctly, are needed. Some artistic skills for retouching color negatives and spotting prints are essential. Keeping detailed records and books for scheduling sittings, planning delivery of finished work, and all financial transactions must be done by somebody at the studio. Often the photographers and their spouses or partners handle most of these tasks until the volume of work justifies hiring additional people.

Purchasing all-new equipment to start a portrait studio is expensive. This type of small business has an unusually high number of failures, so be cautious. Sometimes you can find an established studio that is for sale because the owner is retiring or moving. Purchasing an existing facility with most of the equipment you will need, and a list of customers, often can be the best way for a younger photographer to get started. Check the classified ads in the back of publications such as *The Professional Photographer*, *The Rangefinder*, and *Studio Photography and Design* for current listings of studios and equipment for sale.

If you decide to open a studio of your own, try to have adequate capital to stay in business for a year or more with minimal additional income. It takes time to become established and pay all the monthly bills as well as have some left over for a salary for yourself.

Portraiture with the 35mm Camera

For each picture-making situation and for each photographer, there is a format that is appropriate to the creation of the ideal image. Alfred Eisenstadt, a pioneer in the use of the 35mm camera, was the first of many who responded to the particular possibilities of this format to make exciting, alive portraits.

The advantages of 35mm portraiture are:

- **Size.** The relatively small size of the camera means easy portability and availability for location and informal portraiture.
- **Flexibility.** The variety of lenses available, their easy interchangeability, and the greater number of exposures per loading encourage creative exploration.
- **Ease of use.** The relatively greater depth of field of shorter lenses means that photographs can be made with less light.

Print size (extreme enlargements) and quality used to be considered limitations of the 35mm format. However, today's materials and the capabilities that many laboratories have for the production of large prints have minimized these problems.

The 35mm camera can be used in a portrait studio in place of a view camera, but it is in environmental situations that the 35mm presents the greatest opportunities for unique portraiture. The subject can be actively involved with the photographer and can be captured on film as the real individual he or she is, without the dissimulation that often occurs in formal, camera-on-tripod situations. The photojournalistic portrait is an obvious example. Executive portraits appearing in annual reports and other corporate publications are often done with a 35mm camera, portraying people in actual situations to convey spontaneity and credibility. The 35mm is also a natural for informal portraits of children and the tool par excellence for character studies and travel photos.

One caution: a simple fun-and-games, "click-click" approach will produce only sloppy snapshots. The fundamental requirements of appropriate lighting, good composition, and control of the image are the same for 35mm as for larger formats. Even when unable to manipulate the subject, light, and location, the photographer must be aware of everything in the picture area. He or she also must be so familiar with the equipment that the mechanical aspects are automatic, permitting concentration on the aesthetics of the picture and interaction with the subject in a natural manner. The results can be strong images—portraits full of life and reality.

Reference Sources

Photographic supply salespersons, representing dozens of companies anxious to make new contacts for sales and service, are good sources of helpful information on where to get firsthand advice from the most successful people in the profession. The names of these men and women are easy to find. Just ask a professional photographer who has an established business location.

The publications in the Recommended Reading section and organizations in Appendix A of this book are also good sources for more information. An increasing amount of product information, including objective reviews, is also available on the Internet.

It is always a good idea to read as much as you can about the features of any type of photographic equipment prior to purchasing new items. Reading what publications have to say is a good practice for anybody who will be using the equipment.

6

SCIENTIFIC, TECHNICAL, AND INDUSTRIAL PHOTOGRAPHY

THIS CHAPTER EXPLORES the areas of scientific, technical, and industrial photography. Each area is unique in its own right. You would be surprised at how easy it is to marry numerous areas of interest into one lucrative career. For example, if you're interested in anatomy and physiology as well as taking pictures, you can find work in biomedical photography. If you've always admired the police force and thought of becoming a cop, but would also like to put your photo skills to work, you could be an evidence or forensic photographer. Read on to discover other exciting options in scientific, technical, and industrial photography.

Scientific and Technical Photography

Scientific and technical aspects of photography are difficult to define, since they are diversified and include both picture-making and non-picture-making skills and activities. A random sampling of individuals doing technical photography work disclosed that there were more than 250 job titles that covered this aspect of photography.

Picture-making aspects of this exciting, broad field include high-speed photography, lasers, electron microscopes, holograms, stroboscopes, high-speed film, video cameras, photomacrography, photomicrography, color photography, and color printing. An individual with a background and experience in this field, which normally requires advanced education plus considerable on-the-job training, could work primarily in non-picture-making activities. These include technical writing, laboratory supervision, product development and testing, sales, or technical representation for manufacturers of photographic equipment and materials.

Academic training in this discipline is not available everywhere. The Rochester Institute of Technology offers both two-year A.A.S. and four-year B.S. degrees in imaging and photographic technology among the seven subject areas offered in undergraduate photographic courses. There are relatively few picture-making courses in this program; instead, it is mainly science-engineering in emphasis. The number of graduates is relatively small, but there is a considerable demand for individuals with this type of training, so graduates often receive high starting pay compared to other branches of photography. Other schools and colleges offer courses in various aspects of scientific and technical photography; check catalogs or program brochures for details.

Professional Associations

The following paragraphs describe several unique societies and professional associations worth researching if you're interested in scientific and technological photography. Even if you don't choose to join one such organization, you may find a wealth of information on their websites or in reading the various journals that are published by each. Benefits of membership are usually greater but it may also be expensive, and you may need to possess some kind of degree as criteria for membership.

Society for Imaging Science and Technology

According to the Society for Imaging Science and Technology (imaging.org), "There are two directions you can take in photographic sciences. You can work in the application of photography to the needs of industry, medicine, and government. Or you can carry out pure research aimed at the discovery and control of the basic elements of photography."

The Society for Imaging Science and Technology has several technical sections within its membership, concentrating on special areas of photography. It also hosts conferences and publishes two journals—the *Journal of Electronic Imaging* and the *Journal of Imaging Science and Technology.*

For further information contact the Society for Imaging Science and Technology at the address provided in Appendix A.

International Society for Optical Engineering

The broad range of subjects represented by the International Society for Optical Engineering (spie.org) is an indication of many more kinds of imaging a student may consider as a career:

Biomedical research	Earth resources
Cartography	Electronic imaging
Coherent optics	Electro-optical systems

Environmental quality
Fiber optics techniques
High-speed photography
Holography
Image enhancement
Image processing
Infrared measurements
Laser applications
Micrography
Multispectral sensing
Optical communications
Optical data reduction

Optical systems design
Pattern recognition
Photographic data
   recording
Photo-optical materials
Range instrumentation
Space optics
Transportation studies
Underwater photography
Underwater research
X-ray

It also publishes the *Optical Testing Digest*. For more information, contact the International Society for Optical Engineering at the address listed in Appendix A.

American Society for Photogrammetry and Remote Sensing

Photogrammetry, as defined by the American Society for Photogrammetry and Remote Sensing (asprs.org), is the "art, science, and technology of obtaining reliable information about physical objects and the environment through processes of recording, measuring, and interpreting photographic images and patterns of electromagnetic radiant energy and other phenomena."

An important application of photogrammetry has been the compilation of topographic maps and surveys, complete with contour lines, based on measurements and information obtained from aerial and space photographs.

Another application of photogrammetry is called remote sensing, in which an image is recorded by means of electronic scanning, microwaves, radar, or by thermal infrared, ultraviolet, and multi-spectral sensors. Remote-sensing imagery is used for the production of conventional maps, thematic maps, and resource surveys.

In addition to topographic mapping, photogrammetry is used in aerospace, agriculture, archaeology, architecture, dentistry, engineering, forestry, geology, medicine, oceanography, and urban planning in such diverse applications as highway and traffic studies, ecological studies, military science, structural analysis, and anatomy studies. Employment possibilities exist in federal, state, provincial, and local government organizations; educational institutions; and private industry.

Persons desiring to become career photogrammetrists should acquire a fundamental background in physical mathematics in addition to scientific and technical subjects. The professional photogrammetrist is usually a college graduate who develops practical knowledge through experience and continuing education. Technicians complete high school and usually attend technical colleges for additional training.

Remote sensing and photogrammetry are an integral part of many programs at colleges and universities in the United States and Canada. Course titles include Photointerpretation, Photogeology, Astrogeology, Photogrammetry, and Image Processing.

For further information on careers in photogrammetry, contact the American Society for Photogrammetry and Remote Sensing at the address listed in Appendix A.

Biomedical Photography

One of the most exciting careers in photography today is in the field of biomedical photography. Medical schools, hospitals, research institutions, and veterinary facilities offer the biomedical photographer a great deal of diversity in job opportunities.

The scope of biomedical photography does not limit the types of photographs you will take. The biomedical photographer does nature, field, public relations, portrait, and copy photography. In addition to these basic tasks, the photographer also photographs patients and operating room procedures, produces photomicrographs, and is involved in television production.

To work in this area, the biomedical photographer must have a thorough knowledge of photography as well as a basic understanding and interest in the medical and biological sciences. Training in the use of computers and computer graphics is important.

Photographs produced by biomedical photographers are used in a variety of ways. Some are used in scientific research and medical education, while others are published in journals or brochures or displayed at scientific conferences and seminars. Obviously, the biomedical photographer has a unique opportunity to contribute both to the field of photography and to advancements in the fields of medical and biological science.

If you are interested in this branch of photography, visit a local hospital, medical school, or research institution that has photographic facilities so you can see firsthand what the job is all about.

In the past, biomedical photographers prepared for their careers through on-the-job training. Now several schools throughout the United States offer formal programs that lead to either associate degrees or bachelor's degrees in biomedical photography. Some schools also offer master's degree–level courses in the area of biomedical communications. These courses cover such areas as communication and educational theory and broaden the scope of the photographer's production skills.

The biomedical photographic communications program at the Rochester Institute of Technology (RIT) provides a curriculum leading to a bachelor of science degree. The program is designed to prepare the student for a career in media production within the scientific community. Typical courses include the following:

Biomedical Photography I and II
Survey of Biomedical Photography
Color Printing
Preparation of Biomedical Visuals
Medical Terminology
Digital Photography
AV Production
Liberal arts core courses

The biomedical photographer can be part of allied health teams in hospitals, medical and dental research centers, or in other health institutions. The Biocommunications Association (formerly Biological Photographic Association) has cooperated with RIT in development of the biomedical photography program, which can provide the educational background to qualify as a registered biological photographer (RBP) after the student enters into the profession full-time.

In addition to the formal education available in school, the Biocommunications Association (bca.org) sponsors two one-week workshops in biomedical photography. The BPA also conducts a registration program for those who want to be recognized as competent in the area of biomedical photography. To become a registered biological photographer, you must undergo the BPA's three-part program, which consists of a written examination, a series of practical examinations, and an oral examination.

Lists of schools teaching biomedical photography can be obtained by writing to the Biocommunications Association at the address listed in Appendix A.

Photography in Law Enforcement

Law enforcement photography is a challenge—as great a challenge as the process of solving crimes. Learning all the ways photography can be used in law enforcement provides an endless source of work and study for the proficient photographer, as well as for the investigators who depend upon photography to document evidence.

An organization dedicated to bettering evidence photography both in and out of law enforcement is the Evidence Photographers International Council (epic-photo.org). EPIC developed a formal Standard for Crime Scene Photography that makes simple and orderly the approach to the law enforcer's difficulties. EPIC has stated its belief that if the standard could be adopted nationwide by all law enforcement agencies, the rate of convictions in the courts would increase dramatically.

The civil side of forensic photography supports many photographers. Their expertise varies from the simplest concept of picture-snapping to sophisticated work with excellent equipment. It seems inevitable that this group will increase, although opportunities are scarce for instruction and training.

One specialty of great interest is that of the examiner of questionable documents. Some workers seem attracted to this discipline, possibly because it demands constant effort to keep up with developments in detection methods.

EPIC is planned after the pattern of the British Qualifying Associations in that it allows serious workers to submit to an honors program. If successful, the candidate may obtain either an associateship or a fellowship in evidence photography. This citation is increasingly accepted in the courts as part of the qualifying procedures to serve as expert photographic witnesses under the rules and regulations of United States courts.

EPIC membership is open to qualified persons. Annual membership dues cover the cost of the *Journal of Evidence Photography*. See Appendix A for contact information.

Industrial Photography

Businesses and industrial concerns often have enough year-round photographic work to justify having internal photographic departments. (Departments range in size from one person to several hundred; they are usually related to the size of the company and its use of photography.) Sometimes the products photographed are so large, or secret, that the firm does not want outsiders to see the product. Uses of the photographs are many. They might be very technical, complex analysis photos for engineering research and development, records of processes and equipment, or publicity or advertising photos. All types of equipment are used: conventional color and black-and-white stills from 35mm to 8 × 10; high-speed analysis films; videotapes; stills made from digital cameras, videos, and slides; and photo-resist and high-contrast lithography.

The industrial photographer is usually a very versatile individual. Assignments can include every aspect of commercial photography, as well as portrait and illustration. Characteristics of a good industrial photographer include:

- **Competence**—must be an extremely good technician
- **Versatility**—must be able to handle a large variety of assignments

- **Imagination**—must be able to bring variety and interest to everyday assignments

Advantages and Disadvantages

Working situations in industrial photography are quite different from those in commercial or portrait photography. Most companies keep a 40-hour week with regular and predictable hours. However, last-minute overtime is common to get projects completed.

Most industrial photographers are paid on an hourly basis. Department managers and the top photographers are sometimes salaried. In general, the pay rates of industrial photographers are the best in the photographic field. In addition to salaries, many fringe benefits are usually provided. Company cars, pension and profit sharing, retirement benefits, paid vacation time, health insurance, and sick leave are benefits that may be offered by large companies. Only some of these benefits would be available in the small photographic studios. There are often opportunities to travel for work, but this is often not as glamorous as it sounds. A photographer, when traveling, must contend with a hard schedule, the possibility of illness in strange surroundings, and getting cases of equipment through security at airline terminals.

One disadvantage of industrial photography is sometimes slower career advancement as compared with what is typical in a commercial photographic operation. Also, many companies have dress codes and business dress is sometimes required. The hours that must be kept are strictly enforced, and people who do not have good on-time and attendance records usually don't last very long. In most companies, photography is not a full-time business, so the photographer may have less stature in the company than others who are directly involved in the production of a product.

All in all, though, the industrial or corporate photographer is usually well paid and enjoys good equipment and working conditions.

Job Preparation

The best qualification for obtaining a job in industrial photography is a degree from a recognized college or university. The course of study should include a large amount of technical photography, photo lab technology, and basic video, as well as artistic and design courses. Experience in any kind of photography, in addition to training, is also a plus.

Most beginning jobs are specialized, such as processing and laboratory work, but advancement does require the ability to be flexible and versatile. Each company has its own unique photographic requirements, and most departments are specifically designed to meet these needs.

Getting Started

There is no clear-cut, tried-and-true method of obtaining a position as an industrial photographer. Some of the methods are obvious, such as looking in newspapers, trade periodicals, and employment websites for help-wanted ads or knocking on doors at companies that have a photographic department. Registering with employment agencies also produces results occasionally. Most often, job openings are created by expanded workloads or the need to replace people who are leaving. Most people are hired through the company's personnel department. Many positions are filled through contacts made in local photographic associations and affiliates of the Professional Photographers of America.

7

CAREERS IN
PHOTOJOURNALISM

THIS IMPORTANT ASPECT of photography includes work done for
newspapers and magazines, websites, wire services, and other
instances where the photographer records everyday events for publication. An excellent description of a photojournalist was written
by the late Arthur Rothstein in his book *Photojournalism*, published
by Amphoto:

> Photojournalists are the observers of people and events who report
> what is happening in photographs; interpreters of facts and occur-
> rences who write with a camera; skilled communicators whose
> images are transmitted visually via the printed page. Their audi-
> ence consists of the readers of newspapers and magazines all over
> the world. Their subject is this planet and its inhabitants in all
> aspects, for the photographic image speaks directly to the mind
> and transcends the barriers of language and nationality.

Aptitudes Needed in Photojournalism

In the field of photojournalism, academic education alone will not be enough to prove that you have what it takes. A photojournalist must be strong enough physically, mentally alert at all times, eager, and willing to go anywhere on a moment's notice and come back with pictures that tell the story, regardless of the conditions encountered. In this business, competition is keen among the top names—the picture comes first and the photographer comes in a close second. Many a camera has been smashed and many an injury inflicted upon photographers while doing their duty to get pictures of top news-breaking stories of riots, floods, strikers' picket lines, celebrities, sporting events, and wars. Even when the editor of the newspaper or the news director senses the possibility that danger is involved, the photographer often arrives on the scene without knowing all the facts and starts making pictures despite the risks.

Competent photographers realize that top quality and good composition have to coexist with tight deadline pressure. While the commercial photographer has to keep a top-notch business going, the photojournalist has to go one better, as far as speed and meeting deadlines are concerned. A matter of even five minutes—given today's rapid picture processing and picture transmissions via the Internet and satellite—could mean the difference of a "scoop" by a competing paper, TV station, or website. This five-minute scoop could mean that the whole nation would first learn of the big news break because of one photographer's alertness and speed.

The mood, atmosphere, and conditions existing at the time an event occurs have to be recorded in a hurry with a digital camera, a 35mm camera and film, or videotape by the photojournalist. In other words, he or she is a reporter with a camera. The photographer will not be able to rewrite the story, as the reporter can do. The photographer must take the attitude that "it is now or never" and make a practice of thinking this way even on routine assignments. Bill Strode, a national newspaper photographer of the year, once said, "I tackle my routine assignments as if they were assignments of national importance." Another name press photographer said, "When you tackle a new assignment in the same old way, you are beaten before you get started." A lesson to be learned in photojournalism is that in this business, you have to always be alert and use good common sense and judgment to come back with the picture story.

Meeting important people—whether in the fields of public affairs, sports, or entertainment—and being an eyewitness to the breaking of top news stories is exciting and glamorous when reading about it. However, having to go on a moment's notice to do an assignment and not knowing the conditions under which you will be working can become a little tiresome. Being away from your family, going into dangerous places, and being exposed to diseases and severe weather conditions are all things to take into consideration when choosing photojournalism as a career. One only has to follow the marvelous pictures in *National Geographic*, *Time*, *Newsweek*, *Sports Illustrated*, the daily newspapers, and on television to see how important a medium photography is in today's communications.

Keeping Current

To become more knowledgeable about the photojournalism field, it would be well worth your time to visit the nearest daily newspaper photographic department and inquire about the dates of future workshops and photography exhibitions scheduled in your state. The most famous one is the annual National Press Photographers Association Flying Short Course (search on nppa.org), which is typically offered in five different locations each year—sometimes in cities and sometimes on college campuses. Photographic exhibitions, and many times the programs, presented by outstanding television, magazine, and press photographers, are open to interested outsiders by paying the registration fee. Attending the courses keeps one up to date on the latest techniques and affords the opportunity to talk directly with top photographers.

Most colleges have evening photographic classes and workshops scheduled through their continuing education departments. Also, check with photo supply stores for the dates of other industry courses.

Equipment Used

As to the amount of equipment needed for coverage of photo stories and news photographs, the press and magazine photographer has a slight advantage, with some exceptions, over the television camera operator. It is surprising the amount of work that a top-notch news photographer can do with a digital or 35mm camera, a couple of lenses, and a pocketful of 35mm film. However, when going on a planned assignment, he or she may take two or three camera bodies with wide-angle, normal, and long focal length lenses; color and black-and-white film; and a small electronic flash.

A videographer or cinematographer often is seen with a heavy tripod and a large camera. The equipment is much bulkier and heavier to carry; so is the lighting equipment. Today's portable cameras and lenses are much improved in weight, and modern video cameras are lightweight and shoulder-mounted or handheld, but there is still some extra weight and bulkiness that the movie or television person must handle.

A still photographer normally can find a privately owned studio or darkroom facilities in almost any community where he or she is doing a job to get help in film processing and making a few prints.

A number of sports stadiums in colleges and universities have darkroom facilities, as well as wire-photo transmission rooms, for the photographer who must have immediate processing and transmission equipment.

Ethical Considerations

The role of the photojournalist includes fulfilling a certain measure of public trust. Readers of newspapers, magazines, and books must be able to trust that photos they see are genuine representations of the truth. The same is true of other applications of the photojournalist's work.

The National Press Photographers Association (NPPA) has developed a code of ethics to guide photographers in this area. Members are asked to subscribe to the following:

1. The practice of photojournalism, both as a science and art, is worthy of the very best thought and effort of those who enter into it as a profession.
2. Photojournalism affords an opportunity to serve the public that is equaled by few other vocations, and all members of the profession should strive by example and influence to maintain high standards of ethical conduct free of mercenary considerations of any kind.
3. It is the individual responsibility of every photojournalist at all times to strive for pictures that report truthfully, honestly, and objectively.
4. As journalists, we believe that credibility is our greatest asset. In documentary photojournalism, it is wrong to alter the content of a photograph in any way (electronically or in the darkroom) that deceives the public. We believe the

guidelines for fair and accurate reporting should be the criteria for judging what may be done electronically to a photograph.

5. Business promotion in its many forms is essential, but untrue statements of any nature are not worthy of a professional photojournalist and we condemn any such practice.

6. It is our duty to encourage and assist all members of our profession, individually and collectively, so that the quality of photojournalism may constantly be raised to higher standards.

7. It is the duty of every photojournalist to work to preserve all freedom-of-the-press rights recognized by law and to work to protect and expand freedom of access to all sources of news and visual information.

8. Our standards of business dealings, ambitions, and relations shall have in them a note of sympathy for our common humanity and shall always require us to take into consideration our highest duties as members of society. In every situation in our business life, in every responsibility that comes before us, our chief thought shall be to fulfill that responsibility and discharge that duty so that when each of us is finished we shall have endeavored to lift the level of human ideals and achievement higher than we found it.

9. No code of ethics can prejudge every situation, thus common sense and good judgment are required in applying ethical principles.

Corporate Photojournalism

Another photographic specialty is photography for corporate annual reports. These printed and illustrated reports are published for the public as well as for stockholders. Competition for this work is quite high, but the prize often includes an opportunity to do subsequent publications work for corporations.

Some photojournalists find an outlet for their work supplying images to companies for use in PowerPoint presentations and programs. Such programs are shown by corporations and institutions at public gatherings, trade shows, conventions, and sales meetings. In addition to producing photographs for these productions, knowledge of how the programs are put together and familiarization with the mechanics and electronics involved can be valuable.

Sources of Additional Information

Anyone interested in applying for employment as a press photographer with any of the nation's newspapers or news services will find the following sources of information helpful:

Editor and Publisher International Yearbook 2003. New York: Editor and Publisher, 2003; editorandpublisher.com.

General Manager
Associated Press
50 Rockefeller Plaza
New York, NY 10020
ap.org

In addition, many press, television, and wire service photographers belong to the National Press Photographers Association and subscribe to the *News Photographer* magazine (nppa.org). Many magazine photographers are affiliated with the American Society of Media Photographers (asmp.org) and receive its monthly bulletin.

8

RELATED OPPORTUNITIES

THE ABILITY TO use a camera competently does not necessarily make an individual a photographer. Anybody can start a business, but keeping the business flourishing and viable for a number of years is something else. The attrition rate for small businesses of any kind is great, which is why business and marketing know-how, in addition to having a salable skill as a photographer, is imperative.

Competition is keen among people seeking employment as photographers. Each year hundreds of graduates from photography courses are eager to begin their working life as photographers—more job seekers than can possibly be absorbed by the business community. Obviously, the most talented and best-qualified persons will fill the vacant positions.

What about those who do not find employment as photographers? The purpose of this chapter is to list the many positions and job titles other than photographer that are related to the field of photography. We will describe in detail those segments of the imaging industry that offer the greatest number of opportunities. The actual camera work, while indispensable to it, is only one step in the fascinating process of imaging. Many other positions offer challenges and compensations that are equal to, and sometimes greater than, that of photographer. These include, to name just a few: technical and manufacturers' representatives, marketing specialists, public relations specialists, technical writers, equipment maintenance persons, retail salespersons, and, believe it or not, buyers of photography. Art directors at advertising agencies and corporations increasingly are coming from photographic backgrounds.

Specialties and Job Titles

Career opportunities related to still photography, film, the Internet, and television are many and varied. Image-making and audiovisual production represent a great number of different talents and skills. This list was compiled to provide you with an idea of the variety of specialties and job titles in the world of imaging.

AV equipment
  technician
AV programmer
Black-and-white printer
Camera repairer
Cinematographer
Colorist
Director of AV
  communications
Editor of photo
  magazine
Gallery director

Image analyst
Image interpreter
Laboratory assistant
Laboratory technician
Manager of
  photographic services
Marketing specialist in
  photography
Media specialist
Museum curator
Photo interpreter
Photo lab technician

Photo librarian
Photogrammetrist
Photographer's agent
Photographer's assistant
Photographic processing
and finishing manager
Photographic
technologist
Photography director
Picture editor
Picture researcher

Quality control
technician
Quality controller
Retoucher
Studio manager
Stylist
Teacher
Technical writer
Video technician
Videocamera operator
Web photographer

Photographic Processing and Finishing

Working as a photographic laboratory or darkroom technician—processing and finishing photographs—is a true craft that offers many opportunities for those who qualify. Some photography studios will pay as much for a qualified darkroom technician as for a photographer—and some will pay more. The ability to create a fine, finished work of art is rare, as is the person who is not anxious to burst out of the darkroom and try to become a photographer. For those who are willing to spend their working hours completing, and at times improving upon, someone else's photography, the rewards can be quite satisfying.

Professional photographic processing laboratories offer employment opportunities for qualified technicians and managers. These laboratories offer custom services of film processing and printing to professional photography studios and to corporate photographic departments.

Custom enlargement of prints of color originals has become so automated and commonplace today that there is more demand for individuals who can produce quality black-and-white enlargements. There are excellent job opportunities for skilled technicians in this reemerging facet of darkroom work.

Large-scale photofinishing for the amateur market is on the decline due to the introduction of digital cameras. Photofinishing was always a very competitive business, relying on large volumes of work for profitability, and it is even more so now. The processing and printing equipment is very automated with extensive use of electronics. According to *Photo Marketing* magazine, "Photofinishing training has moved into the computer age along with the equipment that itself has become highly computerized."

One-hour minilabs can be found in high-customer-traffic areas all over the country. Such labs are either independently owned or are franchise operations tied in with other minilabs. The processing equipment is compact and automated, so only several people are needed to process the color negative films, make prints, sort the orders, and wait on customers at the counter. Although the manufacturers of the automated processing equipment say that little technical skill is necessary for proper operation of the equipment, some training is imperative.

Students interested in a career in processing and finishing (on both professional/custom and volume amateur levels) should inquire at nearby processing laboratories about possible part-time summer employment. Whenever you have the opportunity to work a few weeks, or months, in any lab or studio, you should do it. There is nothing that will help you decide whether you would like to spend your life working in a specific job as actually doing that type of work for a while. It does not matter if you are just cleaning up the place, mixing chemicals, or doing some other less glamorous job. The experience itself will help you make up your mind about the future.

Photo lab technician skills, both film and digital, still are often learned through on-the-job training, but there are a number of vocational training courses available for this specialty. This type of work is classified as not physically strenuous, but it tends to be very repetitive work done at a rapid pace, and workers are subject to eye fatigue. Work is generally in clean, well-lit areas (especially in the growing number of daylight-operated minilabs), but there is still a small amount of it that is conducted in dimly lit darkrooms. Photo lab work usually involves a 40-hour week.

There are about 60,000 individuals who work as photo lab technicians, with about half of them working for large photofinishing labs. They earn an average salary of about $350 per week, according to the U.S. Department of Labor, although salaries vary and some earn upwards of $600 weekly.

Photo Retailing

Increased sales in the photography industry have emphasized the need for more and better qualified sales and management people. The growing sophistication of consumers and of photo products demands better educated sales and management people to meet the growing economic challenge.

A career in photo retailing can be a lucrative and rewarding step in your future if you have an interest in photography and like to deal with the public, and you have a desire to turn that interest into a profitable future. A successful salesperson can earn the respect of the public and can earn a good financial return as well.

Outside of the major photographic manufacturers' training programs (where one must be a full-time employee to participate), there are a number of short courses and schools with curricula oriented to direct sales techniques. Photographic products and equipment selling requires specialized people to do the job well.

Photo Equipment Technology

A career in photo equipment technology can be profitable and rewarding. Increasingly, knowledge of electronics, especially of microprocessors, is necessary to understand what makes photographic equipment work. A private business devoted to equipment repair and service can be especially profitable.

General service organizations employ service managers, estimators, warranty repair specialists, aerial camera service specialists, designers, and accessory installers. Photographic manufacturers need photo-instrumentation and service specialists, inspectors, estimators, warranty repair technicians, research assistants, service training managers, consumer relations specialists, and quality-control technicians. Distributing and sales organizations predict a steady increase in employment for service managers, field-service representatives, installation technicians, instructors, modification technicians, and customer service managers.

Industry and government opportunities are available as instrumentation specialists, modifications designers and builders, equipment maintenance technicians, test operators, and researchers and consultants. General photo equipment servicing, commercial installations, studio equipment maintenance, identification systems repair, broadcast and nonbroadcast video equipment maintenance, and school visual-aids systems maintenance also offer job opportunities.

The Society of Photo-Technologists (spt.info) promotes technical knowledge in the field of photographic equipment repair and encourages sound operational standards and ethical business practices. For information contact the Society of Photo-Technologists at the address provided in Appendix A.

A number of schools offer courses in camera repair. Today's complex, electronic cameras mean the student must study about both mechanical and electronic workings of cameras. Repair technicians must be able to quickly diagnose problems and make repairs. If you are interested, check with technical schools in your area to see if courses in camera repair are offered or if other related courses might provide some background. Also check with repair shops to see if you can learn on the job.

Photography as Art

Through the years, much has been said and written about the relationship of photography to other art media. The acceptance of photographic exhibits in art museums has made tremendous advancement in recent years in spite of reluctance by some museum officials to devote space and publicity to photography.

A close relationship between art and photography can be traced back to the experiments of Thomas Wedgwood in 1802, when he was inspired by paintings to make his camera exposures. Even Sir Humphry Davy's production of silhouettes could be considered a contribution to the beginning of artistic composition as it is applied to photography.

One of the earliest photographs reproduced strictly for its picturesque quality was "The Open Door," which William Henry Fox Talbot used in *The Pencil of Nature* in 1844. Another early contribution to the use of photography as an illustration medium was when "The Lord's Prayer" was illustrated with a series of ten daguerreotypes by J. J. E. Mayall in 1845. Peter Henry Emerson,

one of the most important nineteenth-century photographers, produced an edition of 200 of his "Life and Landscape of the Norfolk
Broads." In 1973, one of these sets sold for $2,500; three years later
the reported price was close to $22,000.

More recent photographers whose work contributed much to the
elevation of photography as an art were Edward Weston, Walker
Evans, Wynn Bullock, Minor White, Edward Steichen, and Paul
Strand. A print by Ansel Adams that sold for $150 in 1970 would
bring many thousands of dollars today. A leading New York photo
gallery sells prints by contemporary photographers for $150 to
$750. Gallery commissions range from 40 to 60 percent, depend-
ing upon arrangements agreed upon between the gallery and the
photographer.

Today, even top New York City galleries such as Christie's and
Sotheby's regularly conduct photo auctions. Five-figure amounts
for a recognized photographer's work are not uncommon. Rare
photographs have become a routine item at these prestigious galleries. There is a healthy demand for quality photography for display, or as an investment for appreciation in value.

With the development of dye transfer and other direct-color
techniques, color photographic portraiture is hanging in banks,
public buildings, homes, museums, meeting rooms, and the many
other places where oil portraits once predominated. Many fine portrait studios throughout the country are selling large color photographs. Previously, portrait artists working in oil had monopolized
this lucrative business.

Photographs are increasingly used as decoration in business
offices, manufacturing plants, hospitals, restaurants, and other public places. Several professional processing laboratories offer advice
and aid in preparing photographs for decorative purposes.

Federal Government

The majority of the photographers working in the federal government are in the U.S. Air Force, Army, and Navy, as well as in the Departments of Justice, Transportation, Energy, Environmental Protection, Agriculture, Health and Human Services, and Veterans Affairs, and in the National Aeronautics and Space Administration.

Optional photographic fields classified by the U.S. Civil Service Commission include aerial, laboratory, medical, motion picture, scientific and technical, still, television, underwater, and general.

General experience qualifications for federal photographer classifications include experience in operating cameras and related equipment such as still cameras, copy cameras, and 16mm motion picture cameras; carrying out common developing and printing processes and related techniques; or a combination of the two. This general experience must demonstrate increasing ability to exercise artistic ability in selecting, arranging, and lighting the subject; in processing, printing, enlarging, and retouching prints; or both. Advanced photographic training in residence at a technical trade school beyond the high school level or at a recognized college or university can·better qualify you for specialized fields, provided that such training is directly related to the optional field for which application is made.

Applicants are invited to mention any awards, prizes, or commendations received for their photographic work and any publication or exhibition of their photographic work. Samples of photographs may be required to establish eligibility for some positions, but only when specifically requested.

Information and application forms for the above Civil Service positions are available at all post offices.

The Armed Forces

One option is going to one of the military photography schools and utilizing military time to build a good foundation for a lifetime photography career. Some leading photographers got their start in the military service. There is no end to the number of civilian employees working in commercial, industrial, portraiture, photojournalism, and other related fields who received their first photographic training in one of the branches of the military.

The advantage of being able to travel, meet people of other countries and see firsthand how they live, and gain experience with the large variety of cameras and processing equipment the military provides is quite a bargain that should not be overlooked. The major disadvantage, of course, is the risk of being sent into combat or other hazardous situations if a war or military conflict erupts. Military service involves a serious commitment that should not be taken lightly.

A phone call or visit to the recruiting office of your preferred branch of service will give answers to specific questions. Each of the recruiting offices is listed under "U.S. Government" in the telephone directory of large cities and most county seats. School counselors also are supplied with much military material. You can look on the Internet for information, too.

The chances of being assigned to photography in the armed forces would depend on the extent of one's photography education and experience, aptitude tests and interviews, physical examination, changes in photography as a communication medium, and the current demand for photographic personnel.

Military pay and rank advances are governed by acts of Congress and the Defense Department's recommendation. There are stipulations giving hazardous and overseas duty higher rates of pay.

Insurance, education, and veterans' benefits, plus other advantages such as retirement at a younger age than is possible for most persons in business, should not be overlooked when thinking of a possible career in military photography.

Duty in military photography could be anyplace in the world, on ships at sea, at the battlefront, on a submarine exploration trip under the North Pole, on an expedition to the Antarctic, on flights into outer space, in the deserts of the Middle East, or on some remote island.

Film and Television

The motion picture and television fields can provide an interesting and fulfilling career. It takes a great variety of skills to produce a feature film or a major television program. Competition for technical and professional positions is high, especially in Hollywood and New York. Talents range from camera operators to lighting technicians, from animators to film processors and videotape editors.

The glamour of Hollywood and New York will always attract more talent than can possibly be employed. Although we would never presume to discourage a genuine desire to pursue a career in the "big time," you might instead consider a career in corporate or nonbroadcast film and television production.

Opportunities in Teaching

In the past, the teaching of photography was frequently a part-time activity of a professional photographer, who either needed additional income or enjoyed contact with students through the sharing of his or her photographic knowledge. Increasingly, however, teaching became professionalized, until today it is a specific discipline of its own. The emphasis is thus shifting from merely accumulating photographic skills and experiences to a working knowledge of the complex interpersonal behavior we know as teaching. In today's highly competitive job market, it is seldom enough to have only the basic skills and accomplishments of a good photographer; the aspiring teacher must also know how to communicate that information in a way that facilitates the growth of his or her students.

Photography Curricula

There is an increasingly wide variety of ways in which photography is being taught and utilized in contemporary school systems. These ways may be classed as follows:

Vocational

This is usually a two-year program, offered in many community or technical colleges or in trade or vocational schools. Colleges may offer a two-year associate degree or a one-year certificate. Vocational schools will more likely offer some type of certificate that takes a year or less to complete. Typically these programs emphasize the technical aspects of photography, with the purpose of giving the student sufficient job-entry skills to begin making his or her living in the field of commercial, industrial, medical, or portrait photography.

Fine Arts

These programs are generally in either art schools or four-year colleges or universities. The curriculum focuses on the use of photography as an expressive medium, much as drawing, painting, sculpture, dance, or music. In a purely fine arts–oriented program, there is no intent of preparing the student to enter the world of commercial photography, as the primary emphasis is on aesthetics, self-expression, history of the medium, and the relationship of photography to other expressive media.

Multipurpose

Some college, university, and art school programs are large enough to offer a two-track curriculum, with one track leading into commercial applications of photography, and the other track leading in a fine arts direction. Such a program requires a faculty with a very broad background of training and professional experience, which is not frequently found in any one school.

Liberal Arts

This is not usually a full-major program, but rather a series of courses that offer the student a photographic experience without attempting to prepare him or her for a career in photography.

Specialty Programs

Many schools at both the secondary and postsecondary levels have specialty courses in photography designed to fill needs in specific professional areas such as journalism, science, and medicine. These programs, of course, require faculties with very specialized and often extensive training and experience in the specific discipline.

Ancillary Programs

There is a growing awareness on the part of many professional disciplines—from psychotherapy to anthropology—of the necessity of acquiring knowledge of photography. These courses or programs, therefore, are designed for the individual who already has a professional background but who wants to add photographic skills. The teacher in such a program generally needs at least a working knowledge not only of photography, but also of the related professions.

Academic Requirements

Each type or level of school system has its own academic requirements that a teacher must complete to be eligible for employment in the system. There are exceptions to these, but following are the general requirements for each type of system:

Elementary and Secondary Schools

These require an undergraduate degree plus state certification to teach at the appropriate level. Recently, many secondary schools are requiring a master's degree in the area of specialization, if the teacher is to be in charge of a full program.

Community/Technical Colleges

These schools often require the master's degree in the area of specialization, and many systems also require state certification. This is currently the most expansive area of photographic education, both in terms of programs and salaries.

Four-Year Colleges and Universities

There is often a certain amount of flexibility in the requirements for short-term employment at the college level, but tenure usually requires that the faculty member have the terminal degree in his or her area of specialization. In the case of photography, this is the Master of Fine Arts degree (M.F.A.). At one time, this could be completed after the teacher was hired, but with the current large crop of M.F.A. graduates, this practice is no longer as common.

Additionally, the prospective teacher must have demonstrated his or her photographic ability, usually in terms of exhibitions and/or publications.

Vocational Schools

The applied nature of these programs requires that the teacher have professional and commercial experience. Many schools often require that their faculty continue to be active commercially to keep abreast of new developments and practices. Additionally, depending upon the accrediting agency with which the school is affiliated, the faculty also may need an academic degree.

Private Schools

The requirements in private schools at all levels are generally more flexible than those in public or state schools, but this also varies with the requirements imposed by the accrediting body with which the school is affiliated.

Workshops and Alternative Schools

These organizations have the most flexibility of all, with hiring usually based on demonstrated ability and little concern for academic background. This, too, varies with the school or workshop's accreditation. Those institutions that give academic credit to students and participants must meet the same standards as do other credit-awarding institutions.

Personal Qualities

While few individuals possess all the attributes of the "ideal teacher," there are some characteristics that would seem essential for anyone who wishes to teach photography as a career.

The photography teacher—like any other classroom teacher— needs strong group leadership and classroom management skills to efficiently organize her or his classes to carry out the class objectives and goals.

The ideal photography teacher would be a combination carpenter/plumber/electrician/mechanic. With tight school budgets at all levels, the teacher who can work on the myriad problems that occur in even the best photo facilities will be in a much better position to keep a program running smoothly. The photography teacher also must be a budget-maker in most programs, often responsible for large sums spent on supplies and equipment.

The teacher who is also an artist or commercial photographer must learn to work with the inherent conflict of trying to maintain both roles at a professional level of competence. One of the major problems reported by such teachers is the split among their available time, energy, and resources.

Above all, the aspiring teacher must want to work with people. Despite the emphasis in the media on photographic techniques and equipment, photography is done by human beings. Without a genuine respect for the individual student, no meaningful educational dialogue can occur.

Salaries for teaching photography are generally comparable with other arts or professional skills. There is usually no additional compensation for the added responsibilities of teaching a laboratory subject. In some secondary schools, however, there may be additional money for directing a photo club after normal school hours, or advising the student newspaper. Additional outside income may come from judging exhibitions, consulting with other schools, or holding workshops.

Regardless of any other differences of opinion, most photography teachers will agree that theirs is a job that requires long hours—

there is always something more that the conscientious teacher can do. From this standpoint, the photographers who look to a career in teaching to give themselves time to do their own work are likely to be sadly disillusioned. Except for the possibility of usually unpaid summer vacation, the teaching of photography is a full-time job. However, for the man or woman who deeply enjoys working with both photography and people, the teaching of photography can be an eminently satisfying career.

Society for Photographic Education

Many schools now offer courses that result in either Ph.D. or Ed.D. degrees in motion picture, still, or graphic arts photography. Offering such courses are the University of Wisconsin, Northwestern University, New York University, University of New Mexico, University of Oregon, University of Texas at Austin, and University of Southern California. Studying with the goal of becoming a professor of photography may be a wise decision.

The Society for Photographic Education (SPE), an organization of about 1,500 teachers of photography on both the secondary and college levels, was organized to promote high standards of photographic education, to assist members on matters relating to academic freedom, and to increase public awareness of the art of photography.

Most active members are photography instructors with degrees and are full-time employees of leading educational institutions in the United States. Photographic classes taught by SPE members are, in most cases, part of art department curricula and limited to art majors. The classes are normally full, with waiting lists of students hoping to get into the classes the next school term. The curricula are basic and art-related, and they emphasize creativity.

In recent years there has been an increased awareness among SPE members, and among almost all photography studio owners and their professional associations, of the importance of advanced and professional-directed training for preparing graduates for both instructional and professional photography careers. One result has been the increasing number of director of education titles appearing on staff listings of photographic manufacturers and professional photography associations.

For more information about the organization's programs and publications, contact the Society for Photographic Education (spe national.org) at the address listed in Appendix A.

Appendix A

Associations and Societies

Advertising Photographers of America
P.O. Box 1309
Los Angeles, CA 90036
apanational.org

Advertising Photographers of New York
27 W. Twentieth St., Ste. 601
New York, NY 10011
http://apany.com

American Society of Media Photographers (ASMP)
150 N. Second St.
Philadelphia, PA 19106
asmp.org

American Society for Photogrammetry and Remote Sensing
5410 Grosvenor La., Ste. 210
Bethesda, MD 20814
asprs.org

American Society of Picture Professionals
409 S. Washington St.
Alexandria, VA 22314
aspp.org

Association for Educational Communications and Technology
(AECT)
1800 N. Stonelake Dr., Ste. 2
Bloomington, IN 47408
aect.org

Association of Professional Color Imagers
3000 Picture Pl.
Jackson, MI 49201
http://apci.pmai.org

Biocommunications Association
220 Southwind La.
Hillsborough, NC 27278
bca.org

Canadian Association of Journalists
Algonquin College
1385 Woodroffe Ave., #B224
Ottawa K2G 1V8
Ontario
Canada
caj.ca

Canadian Association of Photographers and Illustrators in
 Communications
55 Mill St.
The Case Goods Bldg., Ste. 302
Toronto M5A 3C4
Ontario
Canada
capic.org

Evidence Photographers International Council (EPIC)
600 Main St.
Honesdale, PA 18431
epic-photo.org

International Fire Photographers Association
146 W. Caracas Ave.
Hershey, PA 17033-1510
ifpaonline.com

International Freelance Photographers Organization
P.O. Box 777
Lewiston, NC 27023
aipress.com

International Photographic Historical Organization
P.O. Box 16074
San Francisco, CA 94116
photographyhistory.com

International Society for Optical Engineering
P.O. Box 10
Bellingham, WA 98227-0010
spie.org

National Association of Government Communicators
10366 Democracy La., Ste. B
Fairfax, VA 22030
nagc.com

National Association for Photographic Art
31858 Hopedale Ave.
Clearbrook V2T 2G7
British Columbia
Canada
http://web.idirect.com/~cvdex/napa/napa.html

National Association of Photography Equipment Technologists
c/o PMAI
3000 Picture Pl.
Jackson, MI 49201
pmai.org

National Press Photographers Association, Inc. (NPPA)
3200 Croasdaile Dr., Ste. 306
Durham, NC 27705
nppa.org

North American Nature Photography Association
10200 W. Forty-Fourth Ave., Ste. 304
Wheat Ridge, CO 80033
nanpa.org

Optical Society of America (OSA)
2010 Massachusetts Ave. NW
Washington, DC 20036
osa.org

Photo Marketing Association International (PMAI)
3000 Picture Pl.
Jackson, MI 49201
pmai.org

Photographic Manufacturers and Distributors Association, Inc.
  (PMDA)
109 White Oak La., #72F
Old Bridge, NJ 08857
pmda.com

Photographic Society of America (PSA)
3000 United Founders Blvd., Ste. 103
Oklahoma, OK 73112
psa-photo.org

Professional Photographers of America, Inc.
229 Peachtree St., NE
International Tower
Atlanta, GA 30303
ppa.com

Professional Photographers of Canada, Inc.
1215 Penticton Ave.
Penticton, V2A 2N3
British Columbia
Canada
ppoc.ca

Professional Photographers of Ontario
2833 Donnelly Dr., RR #4
Kemptville K0G IJO
Ontario
Canada
professionalphotographersofontario.com

Professional School Photographers of America
c/o PMAI
1000 Picture Pl.
Jackson, MI 49201
http://pspa.pmai.org

Professional Women Photographers
c/o Photographics Unlimited
17 W. Seventeenth St., 4th Fl.
New York, NY 10011
pwponline.org

Society for Imaging Science and Technology
7003 Kilworth La.
Springfield, VA 22151
imaging.org

Society of Motion Picture and Television Engineers (SMPTE)
595 W. Hartsdale Ave.
White Plains, NY 10607
smpte.org

Society of Photo Finishing Engineers (SPFE)
c/o PMAI
3000 Picture Pl.
Jackson, MI 49201
pmai.org

Society of Photo Technologists (SPT)
1112 S. Spotted Rd.
Cheney, WA 99004
spt.info

Society for Photographic Education (SPE)
110 Art Bldg.
Miami University
Oxford, OH 45056-2486
spenational.org

University Photographers Association of America
c/o Jim Dusen
SUNY Brockport
350 New Campus Dr.
Brockport, NY 14420-2931
upaa.org

Wedding and Portrait Photographers International
P.O. Box 1703
1312 Lincoln Blvd.
Santa Monica, CA 90406
wppinow.com

White House News Photographers Association
7119 Ben Franklin Station
Washington, DC 20044-7119
whnpa.org

Appendix B

Schools

The following schools offer various degrees and certificates in photography.

Certificates and Diplomas

Daytona Beach Community College
1200 W. International Speedway Blvd.
Daytona Beach, FL 32114
dbcc.cc.fl.us

Fanshawe College of Applied Arts and Technology
1460 Oxford St.
London N5Y 5R6
Ontario
Canada
fanshawe.on.ca

Hallmark Institute of Photography
P.O. Box 308
Turners Falls, MA 01376
http://hallmark.edu

New England School of Photography
537 Commonwealth Ave.
Boston, MA 02215
nesop.com

New York Institute of Photography
211 E. Forty-Third St.
New York, NY 10017
nyip.com

Ohio Institute of Photography and Technology
2029 Edgefield Rd.
Dayton, OH 45439
oipt.com

A.A. or A.S. Degrees

Academy of Art College
79 New Montgomery
San Francisco, CA 94108
academyart.edu

Ampro Photography School
636 E. Broadway
Vancouver V5T IX6
British Columbia
Canada
ampro-photo.com

Antonelli College
124 E. Seventh St.
Cincinnati, OH 45202
antonellic.com

Antonelli Institute
2910 Jolly Rd.
Plymouth Meeting, PA 19462
antonelli.org

Art Institute of Fort Lauderdale
1799 SE Seventeenth St.
Fort Lauderdale, FL 33316
aifl.edu

Art Institute of Houston
1900 Yorktown St.
Houston, TX 77056
aih.aii.edu

Art Institute of Philadelphia
1622 Chestnut St.
Philadelphia, PA 19103
aiph.artinstitutes.edu

Art Institute of Pittsburgh
526 Penn Ave.
Pittsburgh, PA 15222
aip.aii.edu

Art Institute of Seattle
2323 Elliott Ave.
Seattle, WA 98121
ais.edu

Ball State University
Muncie, IN 47306
bsu.edu

Brigham Young University
Provo, UT 84602
http://home.byu.edu

Brooks Institute
801 Alston Rd.
Santa Barbara, CA 93108
brooks.edu

Chowan College
200 Jones Dr.
Murfreesboro, NC 27855
chowan.edu

Colorado Institute of Art
200 E. Ninth Ave.
Denver, CO 80203

Daytona Beach Community College
1200 W. International Speedway Blvd.
Daytona Beach, FL 32114
dbcc.cc.fl.us

DeAnza College
21250 Stevens Creek Blvd.
Cupertino, CA 95014
deanza.fhda.edu

Ferris State College
901 S. State
Big Rapids, MI 49307
ferris.edu

Hallmark Institute of Photography
P.O. Box 308
Turners Falls, MA 01376
http://hallmark.edu

Hawkeye Community College
1501 E. Orange
Waterloo, IA 50701
hawkeye.cc.ia.us

Institute Fontecha
De Tierra Station
San Juan, PR 00906

Kilgore College
1100 Broadway
Kilgore, TX 75662
kilgore.edu

Lansing Community College
419 N. Capitol Ave.
Lansing, MI 48901
lansing.cc.mi.us

Louisiana Art Institute
7380 Exchange Pl.
Baton Rouge, LA 70806

Milwaukee Area Technical College
700 W. State St.
Milwaukee, WI 53223
milwaukee.tec.wi.us

New England School of Photography
357 Commonwealth Ave.
Boston, MA 02215
nesop.com

Paler College of Art
20 Gorham Ave.
Hamden, CT 06517

Phoenix College
1202 W. Thomas Rd.
Phoenix, AZ 85035
pc.maricopa.edu

Rochester Institute of Technology
Rochester, NY 14623
rit.edu

School of Communication Arts
2526 Twenty-Seventh Ave. S
Minneapolis, MN 55406
sca3d.com

SUTECH School of Vocational Technical Training
34277 E. Olympic Blvd.
Los Angeles, CA 90023

University of Bridgeport
126 Park Ave.
Bridgeport, CT 06601
bridgeport.edu

Western Academy of Photography
755A Queens Ave.
Victoria, BC V8T 1M2
Canada

B.A. or B.S. Degrees

Arizona State University
Tempe, AZ 85287
asu.edu

Ball State University
Muncie, IN 47306
bsu.edu

Boston University
1 Sherborn St.
Boston, MA 02215
bu.edu

Brigham Young University
Provo, UT 84602
http://home.byu.edu

Brooks Institute
801 Alston Rd.
Santa Barbara, CA 93108
brooks.edu

California State University, Fullerton
Fullerton, CA 92834
fullerton.edu

Florida State University
Tallahassee, FL 32306
fsu.edu

Illinois Institute of Technology
3300 S. Federal St.
Chicago, IL 60616
iit.edu

Ithaca College
Roy H. Park School of Communications
Ithaca, NY 14850
ithaca.edu

Kent State University
Kent, OH 44242
kent.edu

Montana State University
Bozeman, MT 59717
montana.edu

Northern Arizona University
Flagstaff, AZ 86011
nau.edu

Northern Michigan University
1401 Presque Isle Ave.
Marquette, MI 49855
nmu.edu

Pennsylvania State University
University Park, PA 16802
psu.edu

The Richard Stockton College of New Jersey
Pomona, NJ 08240
www2.stockton.edu

Rochester Institute of Technology
Rochester, NY 14623
rit.edu

Southern Illinois University
Carbondale, IL 62901
siu.edu

University of Bridgeport
126 Park Ave.
Bridgeport, CT 06602
bridgeport.edu

University of Maryland, Baltimore County
1000 Hilltop Circle
Baltimore, MD 21250
umbc.edu

University of Minnesota
Minneapolis, MN 55435
www1.umn.edu

University of Missouri
Columbia, MO 65211
missouri.edu

University of Wisconsin, Platteville
1 University Plaza
Platteville, WI 53818
uwplatt.edu

B.F.A.

Arizona State University
Tempe, AZ 85287
asu.edu

Boston University
1 Sherborn St.
Boston, MA 02215
bu.edu

Brigham Young University
Provo, UT 84601
http://home.byu.edu

Brooks Institute
801 Alston Rd.
Santa Barbara, CA 93108
brooks.edu

California College of Arts and Crafts
1111 Eighth St.
San Francisco, CA 94107
cca.edu

Central Michigan University
Mount Pleasant, MI 48859
cmich.edu

Colorado State University
Ft. Collins, CO 80523
http://welcome.colostate.edu

Florida State University
Tallahassee, FL 32306
fsu.edu

Indiana State University
200 N. Seventh St.
Terre Haute, IN 47809
indstate.edu

Louisiana Tech University
P.O. Box 3178
Ruston, LA 71272
latech.edu

Memphis College of Art
1930 Poplar Ave.
Overton Park
Memphis, TN 38104
mca.edu

Northern Michigan University
1401 Presque Isle Ave.
Marquette, MI 49855
nmu.edu

Rhode Island School of Design
2 College St.
Providence, RI 02903
risd.edu

Rochester Institute of Technology
Rochester, NY 14623
rit.edu

Southern Illinois University
Carbondale, IL 62901
siu.edu

Syracuse University
Syracuse, NY 13244
syr.edu

Texas Woman's University
Denton, TX 76204
twu.edu

University of Bridgeport
126 Park Ave.
Bridgeport, CT 06602
bridgeport.edu

University of Dayton
300 College Park
Dayton, OH 45469
udayton.edu

University of Rhode Island
10 Chafee Rd.
Kingston, RI 02881
uri.edu

University of Southern California
Los Angeles, CA 90089-0292
usc.edu

University of Texas, Austin
Austin, TX 78712
utexas.edu

University of Wisconsin, Superior
Superior, WI 54880
uwsuper.edu

M.F.A. and Other Master's Degrees

Brooks Institute
801 Alston Rd.
Santa Barbara, CA 93108
brooks.edu

Illinois Institute of Technology
3300 S. Federal St.
Chicago, IL 60616
iit.edu

Louisiana Tech University
P.O. Box 3178
Ruston, LA 71272
latech.edu

Ohio University, Athens
Athens, OH 45701

Rochester Institute of Technology
Rochester, NY 14623
rit.edu

Southern Illinois University
Carbondale, IL 62901
siu.edu

University of Minnesota
Minneapolis, MN 55435
www1.umn.edu

University of New Mexico
Albuquerque, NM 87131
unm.edu

University of Oregon
Eugene, OR 87403

University of Southern California
Los Angeles, CA 90089
usc.edu

University of Texas, Austin
Austin, TX 78712
utexas.edu

Photography Workshops

California

Barbara Brundege Workshops
Summit Photographic Workshops
P.O. Box 67459
Scotts Valley, CA 95067
summitphotographic.com

Michele Burgess Seminars (In Focus with Michele Burgess)
20741 Catamaran La.
Huntington Beach, CA 92646

California Natural Wonders Photography Workshops
P.O. Box 457
La Canada, CA 91012

Lewis Kemper Workshops
3201 Lassen Way
Sacramento, CA 95821
lewiskemper.com

Photo Adventures Workshops
JoAnn Ordano
P.O. Box 591291
San Francisco, CA 94118

Maria Piscopo Workshops
Creative Services Consultant
2038 Calvert
Costa Mesa, CA 92626
mpiscopo.com

David Sanger Workshops
David Sanger
920 Evelyn Ave.
Albany, CA 94706
davidsanger.com

John Sexton Photography Workshops
291 Los Agrinemsors
Carmel Valley, CA 93924
johnsexton.com

West Coast School of Professional Photography Workshops
c/o Professional Photographers of California
138 W. Badilla
Covina, CA 91723
wcschool.com

Wildlife Research Photography Workshops
P.O. Box 3628
Mammoth Lakes, CA 93546-3628
moose395.net

Norbert Wu Workshops
1065 Sinex Ave.
Pacific Grove, CA 93950
norbertwu.com

Youth Outlook (YO!) Photography Workshop
660 Market St., Rm. 210
San Francisco, CA 94104
pacificnews.org/yo/photo

Colorado

Anderson Ranch Arts Center
5263 Owl Creek Rd.
P.O. Box 5598
Snowmass Village, CO 81615
andersonranch.org

Colorado Mountain College Workshops
831 Grand Ave.
Glenwood Springs, CO 81601
coloradomtn.edu

Focus Adventures
Karen Schulman
P.O. Box 771640
555 Pamela La.
Steamboat Springs, CO 80477
photosourcebook.com

Great American Photography Workshops
P.O. Box 357
Windsor, CO 80550
gapweb.com

Florida

Palm Beach Photographic Centre Workshops
55 NE Second Ave.
Delray Beach, FL 33444
workshop.org

Photography in Nature Workshops
Bob Grytten
P.O. Box 3195
Holiday, FL 34690
apogeephoto.com/f8news.html

Shutterbug/PhotoPro Workshops
14419 Chaffee Dr., Suite #1
Titusville, FL 32780
shutterbug.net

Touch of Success Photo Seminars
Bill Thomas
P.O. Box 1436
Dunnellon, FL 34430
http://dontomascreations.com/touchsuccess/southwest.htm

Illinois

Investigative Photography Workshops
Northwestern University
Evanston, IL
northwestern.edu/nucps

Indiana

Charlene Faris Workshops
610 W. Poplar St., Apt. 4
Zionsville, IN 46077-1220
freeagent.com/photobeetle

Kentucky

Gene Boaz Workshops
Nature's Images
1531 Cross Rd.
Route 5
Benton, KY 42025

Maine

Cape Cod Photo Workshops
P.O. Box 1619
North Eastham, MA 02651
http://capecodphotoworkshops.com

Creative Photographic Arts Center of Maine Workshops
Historic Bates Mill Complex
59 Canal St.
Lewiston, ME 04243
aipress.com

Maine Photographic Workshops
P.O. Box 200
2 Central St.
Rockport, ME 04856
theworkshops.com/photoworkshops

Michigan

Gerlach Nature Photography Workshops
John Gerlach
P.O. Box 259
Chatham, MI 49816
gerlachnaturephotography.com

Great Lakes Institute of Photography
c/o Mark I Photography
1201 S. Euclid
Bay City, MI 48706
glip.org

Photo Explorer Tours
2506 Country Village
Ann Arbor, MI 48103-6500
photoexplorertours.com

Minnesota

Vision Quest Photography Workshops
2370 Herndon Ave.
St. Paul, MN 55108
vqphoto.com

Missouri

Missouri Photo Workshop
c/o Jim Curley
University of Missouri
Columbia, MO 65201
mophotoworkshop.org

New Mexico

Santa Fe Workshops
P.O. Box 9916
Santa Fe, NM 87504
sfworkshop.com

New York

Center for Photography at Woodstock Workshops
59 Tinker St.
Woodstock, NY 12498
cpw.org

The Graphic Artists Guild Workshops
90 John St., Ste. 403
New York, NY 10038
gag.org

International Center of Photography
1114 Avenue of the Americas
New York, NY 10028
icp.org

International Museum of Photography and Film
George Eastman House
900 East Ave.
Rochester, NY 14607
eastman.org

New School University Workshops
66 W. Twelfth St.
New York, NY 10011
newschool.edu

New York Institute of Photography Workshops
211 E. Forty-Third St., Dept. WVW
New York, NY 10017
nyip.com

Parsons School of Design Workshops
66 Fifth Ave.
New York, NY 10011
parsons.edu

Rochester Institute of Technology Workshops
P.O. Box 9887
Rochester, NY 14623-0887
rit.edu

Shawguides Workshops
P.O. Box 231295
Ansonia Station
New York, NY 10023
photoworkshops.shawguides.com

Visual Studios Workshop
31 Prince St.
Rochester, NY 14607
vsw.org

North Carolina

Flying Short Courses
National Press Photographers Association
3200 Croasdaile Dr., Ste. 306
Durham, NC 27705
nppa.org

National Press Photographers Association Seminars, Inc.
3200 Croasdaile Dr.
Durham, NC 27705
nppa.org

Oklahoma

Photographic Society of America Regional Seminars
3000 United Founders Blvd., Ste. 103
Oklahoma City, OK 73112
psa-photo.org

Tennessee

Cory Photography Workshops
P.O. Box 42
Signal Mountain, TN 37377
http://hometown.aol.com/tompatcory

Texas

Joe Englander Photography Workshops and Tours
P.O. Box 1261
Manchaca, TX 78652
englander-workshops.com

Vermont

Vermont Photography Workshop
Vermont Center for Photography
49 Flat St.
Brattleboro, VT 05301
vcphoto.org

Wisconsin

Dillman's Sand Lake Lodge Workshops
3305 Sand Lake Lodge La.
P.O. Box 98
Lac du Flambeau, WI 54538
dillmans.com

Rohn Engh's Workshops
Pine Lake Farm
1910 Thirty-Fifth Rd.
Osceola, WI 54020

Recommended Reading

The periodicals and books listed here will give you a good overview of the variety and scope of careers available within the field of photography.

Periodicals

Advertising Age
Crain Communications
711 Third Ave.
New York, NY 10017
adage.com

American Cinematographer
1782 N. Orange Dr.
Los Angeles, CA 90028
theasc.com

Aperture
c/o Aperture Foundation, Inc.
20 E. Twenty-Third St.
New York, NY 10010
aperture.org

Canadian Camera
47 Bunting La.
Ottawa K2M 2P7
Ontario
Canada
http://capa-acap.ca

Computer Graphics World
PennWell
98 Spit Brook Rd.
Nashua, NH 03062
http://cgw.pennet.com

Digital Imaging
445 Broad Hollow Rd.
Melville, NY 11747
cygnusb2b.com

Digital Photo Pro
Werner Publishing Corporation
12121 Wilshire Blvd., 12th Fl.
Los Angeles, CA 90025
digitalphotopro.com

Editor and Publisher
770 Broadway
New York, NY 10003
editorandpublisher.com

Electronic Photography News
10915 Bonita Beach Rd., #1091
Bonita Springs, FL 34135
photo-news.com

Focus on Imaging
1312 Lincoln Blvd.
P.O. Box 1700
Santa Monica, CA 94046
focusonimagingmag.com

Journal of Biocommunications
c/o Gary Lees
Johns Hopkins University
Art as Applied to Medicine
Johns Hopkins School of Medicine
1830 E. Monument St., Ste. 7000
Baltimore, MD 21093
jbiocommunication.org

Journal of Electronic Imaging
IS&T
7003 Kilworth La.
Springfield, VA 22151
imaging.org

Journal of Imaging Science and Technology
IS&T
7003 Kilworth La.
Springfield, VA 22151
imaging.org

News Photographer
c/o NPPA
3200 Croasdaile Dr., Ste. 306
Durham, NC 27705
nppa.org

Outdoor Photographer
12121 Wilshire Blvd., 12th Fl.
Los Angeles, CA 90025
outdoorphotographer.com

PCPhoto
Werner Publishing Corporation
12121 Wilshire Blvd., 12th Fl.
Los Angeles, CA 90025
pcphotomag.com

Petersen's PhotoGraphic Magazine
6420 Wilshire Blvd.
Los Angeles, CA 90048
photographic.com

Photo District News
770 Broadway, 7th Fl.
New York, NY 10003
pdnonline.com

Photo Life
One Dundas St. W, Ste. 2500
P.O. Box 84
Toronto M5G 1Z3
Ontario
Canada
photolife.com

Photo Marketing
Photo Marketing Association International (PMAI)
3000 Picture Pl.
Jackson, MI 49201
pmai.org

Photo Techniques
6600 W. Touhy Ave.
Niles, IL 60714
phototechmag.com

Photographic Processing
445 Broad Hollow Rd.
Melville, NY 11747
imaging-info.com

Popular Photography and Imaging
1633 Broadway
New York, NY 10019
popphoto.com

The Professional Photographer
c/o PPofA
229 Peachtree St. NE, Ste. 2200
International Tower
Atlanta, GA 30303
ppmag.com

The Rangefinder
1312 Lincoln Blvd.
P.O. Box 1703
Santa Monica, CA 90406
rangefindermag.com

Shutterbug
1419 Chaffee Dr., Ste. #1
Titusville, FL 32780
shutterbug.net

Studio Photography and Design
c/o PTN Publishing Company
445 Broad Hollow Rd.
Melville, NY 11747
imaging-info.com

Today's Photographer
P.O. Box 777
Lewisville, NC 27023-0777
aipress.com

View Camera
P.O. Box 2328
Corrales, NM 87048
viewcamera.com

The Wedding Photographer
1312 Lincoln Blvd.
Santa Monica, CA 90406
wppinow.com

Wildlife Photography
5435 Briarfield Rd.
Jackson, MS 39211
wildlifephoto.net

Books

ASMP. *ASMP Professional Business Practices in Photography*, 6th ed. New York: Allworth Press, 2001.

Bidner, Jenni. *Digital Photography: A Basic Guide to New Technology*. Rochester, N.Y.: Silver Pixel Press, 2000.

Buselle, Julien. *Printing Special Effects*. Rochester, N.Y.: Silver Pixel Press, 2000.

———. *Processing and Printing*. Rochester, N.Y.: Silver Pixel Press, 2000.

Cantrell, Bambi, Skip Cohen, and Denis Reggie. *The Art of Wedding Photography*. New York: Watson-Guptill Publications, 2000.

Crawford, Tad. *Business and Legal Forms for Photographers*, 3rd ed. New York: Allworth Press, 2002.

Curtin, Dennis, Joe DeMaio, and Roberta Worth. *The New Darkroom Handbook*. Burlington, Mass.: Focal Press, 1997.

Curtin, Dennis and Steve Musselman. *Into Your Darkroom Step by Step*, rev. ed. Buffalo, N.Y.: Amherst Media, 1991.

Duboff, Leonard D. *The Law, in Plain English, for Photographers*, rev. ed. New York: Allworth Press, 2002.

Ephraums, Eddie. *Creative Exposures: 23 Photographers Discuss Art and Technique*. Rochester, N.Y.: Silver Pixel Press, 2000.

Farace, Joe. *Part-Time Glamour Photography—Full-Time Income*. Rochester, N.Y.: Silver Pixel Press, 2000.

———. *The Photographer's Internet Handbook*, rev. ed. New York: Allworth Press, 2001.

Fell, Derek. *Flower and Garden Photography*. Rochester, N.Y.: Silver Pixel Press, 2000.

Heron, Michal, and David MacTavish. *Pricing Photography: The Complete Guide to Assignment and Stock Prices*, 3rd ed. New York: Allworth Press, 2002.

Hope, Terry. *Landscapes: Developing Style in Creative Photography*. Rochester, N.Y.: Silver Pixel Press, 2000.

————. *Portraits and Figures: Developing Style in Creative Photography*. Rochester, N.Y.: Silver Pixel Press, 2000.

Kodak. *Kodak Black and White Darkroom Dataguide*, 6th ed. Rochester, N.Y.: Silver Pixel Press, 2001.

————. *Kodak Guide to 35mm Photography*. Rochester, N.Y.: Silver Pixel Press, 2000.

————. *Kodak Pocket Guide to Digital Photography*. Rochester, N.Y.: Silver Pixel Press, 2000.

Krages, Bert P. *Legal Handbook for Photographers: The Rights and Liabilities of Making Images*. Buffalo, N.Y.: Amherst Media, 2001.

Lemon, Bill. *Professional Secrets of Nude and Beauty Photography*. Buffalo, N.Y.: Amherst Media, 2001.

Peterson, B. Moose. *Nikon Lenses*, 2nd ed. Rochester, N.Y.: Silver Pixel Press, 2000.

————. *Nikon System Handbook*, 6th ed. Rochester, N.Y.: Silver Pixel Press, 2000.

Pinkard, Bruce. *The Nude: Complete Photography Course*. Rochester, N.Y.: Silver Pixel Press, 2000.

Piscopo, Maria. *The Photographer's Guide to Marketing and Self-Promotion*, 3rd ed. New York: Allworth Press, 2001.

Sedge, Michael. *The Photojournalist's Guide to Making Money*. New York: Allworth Press, 2000.

About the Authors

Bervin Johnson's work in the publication, commercial, industrial, portrait, freelance, and photography education fields has earned him national recognition as a photographer, exhibition judge, and educator, as well as the Qualified Professional Photographer rating from the Professional Photographers of America.

For 17 years he operated his own freelance photography business, doing assignments and furnishing stock photographs for many of the nation's largest advertising agencies and for industrial and publishing firms. His photographs and writings have been published throughout the United States and abroad while working for the *Oklahoma City Times* and *Oklahoman, Dayton Journal-Herald, Sarasota Herald-Tribune, Birmingham News-Age-Herald, Atlanta Georgian,* and the Associated Press Southern Bureau. He is a charter life member of the National Press Photographers Association (NPPA) and the Michigan chapter of the NPPA, and a life member of the Professional Photographers of America. He was a Michigan State University student adviser and supervised on-the-job training in photojournalism before he resigned to travel full-time for five years—to do a travelogue on Magic Wonders of America.

Bob Mayer's interest in photography started while attending high school in Columbus, Ohio, where he was active in the camera club. Evenings and for two summers he worked for a local photofinisher. During six years' active duty in the U.S. Air Force, Mayer worked in base photo labs and in aerial photo reconnaissance labs. He then obtained both B.F.A. and M.F.A. degrees in photography from Ohio University. He worked in industrial photo studio management for several photographic manufacturers for more than 17 years. During this time he lectured on photography all over the United States.

Mayer has taught photography at both Rochester Institute of Technology (RIT) and Arizona State University, and for many years he has been involved with teaching and coordinating short courses and workshops. He was a consultant on five volumes of the original Life Library of Photography. Currently a freelance writer/photographer, he is a contributing editor for *Shutterbug* and *Photomethods* magazines, where he has authored numerous feature articles on various photographic subjects and helps write monthly question-and-answer columns. He writes regularly for other publications, including *Law and Order* and *Photo Lab Management*. His professional guidebook on the Minolta Maxxum "i" series of cameras was published in 1991 by Hove Foto Books.

Fred Schmidt spent the first 18 years of his life in Lone Wolf, Oklahoma, and environs. After service in the U.S. Coast Guard in World War II, he became interested in photography. He attended the Chicago School of Photography and began his career as an assistant photographer in a commercial studio there. Schmidt worked on several early television commercials and later wrote a column on color photography for *The National Photographer* magazine. He joined the Professional Photographers of America in 1955 and served as editor of *The Professional Photographer* for several years. In 1974 he was appointed editor of *Photomethods* magazine, a position he held for well over ten years.

Schmidt has been a guest lecturer in many high school and college photography classes; he was a curriculum adviser in photography for the Milwaukee Area Technical College. He also has organized and taught photography and electronic imaging courses.